a little
more wine

a little more wine

father paul f. halloran

sister ramona schweich, ssnd

Cover Design by R. G. Davis

Printed at St. Mary's College Press, Winona, Minnesota

A Little More Wine
©1977 by Father Paul F. Halloran
Printed in the United States of America

Contents

vintage '69   1

vintage '70   73

vintage '71   137

foreword

The most difficult part of the book to write is the Foreword. Therein a person is expected to make statements concerning purpose and meaning. When this book was written there wasn't any specific reason for writing it except to share a few thoughts with friends and would-be friends in Jesus Christ.

I can only add to that the fact that Sister Ramona has been a friend since 1957. Through reading her comments throughout the book I have come to know her beautiful personality and character more completely.

Each short essay I wrote was with the Lord in mind. Through her responses I have found another Christ in her. She is a patient Christ, an understanding Christ, a suffering Christ.

In *A Little Wine* many found strength and consolation in Sister's remarks. Now, in *A Little More Wine*, Sister Ramona offers even greater strength and consolation to the sick — and hope for every reader.

Sister's "Remarks" are sterling examples of the weak confounding the strong but they are also an example of a very strong person giving fortitude to the weak.

p.f.h.

in appreciation

Each of us has a list of names that can be classified as our "I admire" column. Most of these "I admire" persons are at the same time people whom we not only respect but are also deeply grateful to for one thing or another.

Periodically perhaps we revise the list and rearrange the names. Within the past several months I've done just that. Since I've been spending so much time going to and from the Mayo Clinic, being diagnosed, and "stuck up" in the Curie Pavilion, my admiration for doctors and nurses has grown and grown.

I dedicate my contribution to this book to all doctors and nurses, who so selflessly spend their lives in health services. More than anyone else I am deeply grateful to Dr. Richard J. Hill of the Mayo staff. Dr. Hill sees me almost every month and with each visit I find him more concerned about me, more gentle and more kind. I am particularly grateful for his ability to "tell me exactly how it is," truthfully, gently and lovingly.

Then, too, there is Dr. Gerald Holcomb, a member of the original team, but a man who still takes time to check me out and to let me know that he follows my case and makes me feel like an individual and not just a clinic card folder number. Each time I see Dr. Holcomb I have a renewed courage to face life as it is.

Dr. Charles Elliott, who is no longer at Mayo, was the man who first stood next to my bed in St. Marys Hospital and whispered, "Sister, we've found that you have lymphoma." I remember so well his expression, his tone of voice and his concern.

The names of Hill, Holcomb and Elliott are respected names for me and they are often whispered in prayer to the Almighty, Who alone has the power to direct and guide all doctors. I am grateful too to the nurses at the Curie Pavilion who see me each month and give me the chemotherapy injections. I know that when the day for that one last visit and that one last injection comes I will still be grateful.

Here at Mankato I have my "at home" doctor whose very presence in town gives me security. The man who gives me security by just being here when I need him for that one last word of hope and confidence is Dr. Al Scheidel. There they are . . . my four men: Hill, Scheidel, Holcomb and Elliott. God bless them, all four.

Sister Ramona Schweich, SSND

vintage '69

Be Attitudes

It never ceases to amaze me that cartoonists, such as the authors of Blondie or Peanuts, can daily produce something so funny. They must be constantly on the alert in their search for material to amuse and teach the reading public.

To produce one good thought a week for the bulletin at times is difficult. Have I said it before—or even worse, has someone else said it earlier and better? Will this be offensive? Will it be interpreted as I intend it? Would it insult someone's intelligence to spell it out more completely—yet be missed completely by some if it is not better spelled out?

Whatever else goes through my mind I am quite constantly trying to come up with ideas concerning Christ and His teachings which can be conveyed to the reader of the bulletin.

Each of us, intent on our business, is ever alert for opportunity to improve ourselves and those about us. In the sermon on the Mount, Our Lord gives us a whole series of means to happiness and blessedness which have, through the centuries, been called the Beatitudes.

If we have an attitude of searching for happiness, we will find it. This must be the daily attitude of the cartoonist. He must enter every episode in life with an effort to derive from it something funny which he can relate to others. Even in misery and sorrow, he must have to think what could have been. And they consistently make us laugh at unfortunate people in difficult circumstances—sometimes by identifying ourselves with the character in distress.

Our Lord's teachings would so easily be brought into our daily life if we would only be aware of the numerous opportunities afforded us. Let us be alert to the happiness of Christ all about us.

Today: I wonder why people aren't as quick about responding to the happiness of Christ around us as they are about laughing at unfortunate people in distress. If we really think about, it seems sad that we often see people laugh when someone else is suffering—when someone is really in distress.

How blessed, on the other hand, to be able to be alert to the real happiness in life—happiness despite pain, fear, oppression, and even the signs of death.

Help me, Lord, to always rejoice with the happiness of Christ and to be as free as the birds and just for good measure throw in the real attitude of joy—pure joy.

Be Attitudes

It never ceases to amaze me that cartoonists, such as the authors of Blondie or Peanuts, can daily produce something so funny. They must be constantly on the alert in their search for material to amuse and teach the reading public.

To produce one good thought a week for the bulletin at times is difficult. Have I said it before—or even worse, has someone else said it earlier and better? Will this be offensive? Will it be interpreted as I intend it? Would it insult someone's intelligence to spell it out more completely—yet be missed completely by some if it is not better spelled out?

Whatever else goes through my mind I am quite constantly trying to come up with ideas concerning Christ and His teachings which can be conveyed to the reader of the bulletin.

Each of us, intent on our business, is ever alert for opportunity to improve ourselves and those about us. In the sermon on the Mount, Our Lord gives us a whole series of means to happiness and blessedness which have, through the centuries, been called the Beatitudes.

If we have an attitude of searching for happiness, we will find it. This must be the daily attitude of the cartoonist. He must enter every episode in life with an effort to derive from it something funny which he can relate to others. Even in misery and sorrow, he must have to think what could have been. And they consistently make us laugh at unfortunate people in difficult circumstances—sometimes by identifying ourselves with the character in distress.

Our Lord's teachings would so easily be brought into our daily life if we would only be aware of the numerous opportunities afforded us. Let us be alert to the happiness of Christ all about us.

Today: I wonder why people aren't as quick about responding to the happiness of Christ around us as they are about laughing at unfortunate people in distress. If we really think about, it seems sad that we often see people laugh when someone else is suffering—when someone is really in distress.

How blessed, on the other hand, to be able to be alert to the real happiness in life—happiness despite pain, fear, oppression, and even the signs of death.

Help me, Lord, to always rejoice with the happiness of Christ and to be as free as the birds and just for good measure throw in the real attitude of joy—pure joy.

The Eyes Have It

Whether it is true or not, the idea was tremendous. The report is that a teacher, at the grade school level, in one of the Twin City schools prepared her pupils for a visit into an area which is predominantly black and poor.

Her preparation was simple, but effective. She checked the eye color of each child in her class and discovered nearly half had brown eyes. Then the teacher had, in turn, those with non-brown eyes deprived of all honors and privileges for one week. They were ignored or cajoled during the same period.

During the second week the brown-eyed children suffered the same treatment at their classmates' hands. The results were drastic and the children split into two definite factions.

Then the entire class visited the deprived area. After being deprived themselves, they were willing to put on old clothes and actually "feel" at home. The teacher had allowed them a rich and rewarding experience.

Isn't it interesting that the children in the classroom had no more control over the color of their eyes than a man of any race has concerning the pigment of his skin.

How idiotic, and consequently un-Christian, can we be to judge a man by that over which is to neither his credit nor blame. Isn't it possible that we should be just as capable of ignoring color of a man's skin as we are the color of his eyes—or better still to recognize the fact that just as any colored eyes can be beautiful—so much more the whole man!

Today: It doesn't take many brains to be prejudiced! All I need
to see *mud* wherever I look is the gift of my eyes.
Because I can see, I can see red, black, brown or white.
I don't even need 20/20 vision. It just dawned on me that
prejudice is one of the results of the fact that human
beings have vision. If I were brave or really virtuous,
I'd pray that God would take my vision rather than allow
me to become a prejudiced "old nun." Instead I'll ask
Him to remove all prejudice from my heart—Lord, let
me "see" but don't let me judge a man because his skin
color differs from mine. We're all God's children.

Blank Slate

One way some people find quite successful in procuring sleep at night when they might otherwise spend hours in fitful tossing and turning, is the use of a blackboard and chalk and eraser. Not real ones, but imagined ones do the trick.

Whatever problem or concern is keeping them awake, one just writes it on the imaginary blackboard, looks at it for a moment, and then erases it. If something else pops up, he repeats the performance. Strangely enough, it works! And one is suddenly asleep.

Unfortunately many of us, somewhat unconsciously, do the same thing in our waking hours. We attend church on Sunday morning. We receive the Eucharist. We hear the sermon. We leave something in the collection box. We might even make a resolution or two if the sermon hits us just right.

Then we hurry home and begin the process of erasing. We devour the Sunday paper. We are transfixed by the pro-football game on television. We become "transformed" by a sumptuous dinner, preceded and followed by a delightful beverage. And if there isn't an interesting movie within fifty miles we return to the TV tube for a few laughs or tears.

After Mass the entire day has been one of erasing. None of the things done are necessarily bad. In fact, it may well be the best possible means of keeping the Sunday rest.

The fact is, though, that on Monday morning one is much more likely to talk about the pro-game than he is about the sermon. He is more likely to remember an anecdote from the Sunday funnies than he is the announcement in the Sunday bulletin.

Maybe the sermon and the bulletins aren't relevant. Maybe the pastor should always save a part of one or the other for predicting the day's scores. Maybe then one would remember on Monday morning how accurately the priest rates the teams. But also—maybe Christ would prefer the priest would continue giving the message of Christ—and not have it erased.

Today: Why are comic strips funnier than parish bulletins??
If they are funnier, they are at least more interesting.
Maybe it's because the pastor at the local church has
lost his sense of humor. Come to think of it, some

clergymen are cartoonists—real humorists—who deeply love Jesus Christ. But the Gospel of Jesus Christ is serious business and we have to thank God that some of them take it seriously.

Some priests bear witness, they spread the good news, but they write dull parish bulletins. Let's pray for them next Sunday as we grab for the funny-paper "after the parish bulletin."

Balance the Books

At the end of the day the banker, the business man or the accountant will balance the books. His work isn't complete until both sides of the ledger equal. Long frustrating hours can be spent in locating a mistake.

Often when one adds the columns, he makes the same mistake each time—and each time the mistake is more easily made and more difficult to catch.

Generally, the problem is the absence of an entry. Until all entries are included the books just won't balance. It is most tedious and most necessary to check each entry; otherwise the answer always comes out incorrectly.

In judging our neighbor the same situation can easily exist. If our initial judgment is in error we continue making the same erroneous judgment with great facility.

Too, when we try to balance our neighbor's books we have a much greater possibility of lacking some pretty important entries rather than possessing them to any degree of fullness. As long as we lack a single entry in another's personality or character or circumstances, how can we possibly arrive at the right answers and balance the books?

Sometimes when the business man is a few cents off he would rather take some coins from his own pocket, balance the books and go home. The business world, however, won't allow such practice.

In the world of judging, when our neighbor's "books" don't seem to balance in our minds, perhaps we are missing too many entries. For a right and just solution we can add our own entries: prayer, kindness and silence—and the books will balance in everyone's favor.

Today: It is easier to check the other guy's books than it is to balance my own. Jesus said something about taking the plank out of my own eye first. Watergate causes all of us to make sure that *no one* "gets in" unless he "paid" and has his books balanced. How unlike Jesus Christ.

Why do my spiritual books have to "balance"? Can't there be more love than hate, more kindness than unkindness? Help me balance my books, O Lord!

Preserve me from a spiritual Watergate! The IR is coming!!!

It's Understood

The family was seated in a relaxed mood around the table after a fine meal. On the back porch the dog was barking furiously and endlessly at the usual nothings. Finally, the mother turned to her husband and asked, "Can't you shut that dog up?"

The father opened the door and with a few well chosen words silenced the family pet. The wife looked at her spouse with a query: "Does that dog understand you?" The husband, resuming his place at the head of the table, answered quite simply, "He is just like everyone else around here. He understands me perfectly but generally disregards me!"

It is obvious that such is too often the case. Children know when there are dishes to be done, floors to be swept and the table to be cleaned. They understand it so well that they quite suddenly disappear at the "opportune" moment. They vanish faster than the angels, and miss the joy of helping.

It doesn't require a Sherlock Holmes to see what needs to be done in a home, but it takes more than him to find someone who will do it. We all understand what should be done and disregard it.

Just as this is the case in the home, so it is in all things. We know pretty well what is right and wrong and what God expects of us. We know what our neighbor expects of us—and we know what we can do when we are tempted to disregard it all.

To understand God's will, neighbor's will, and our own honest will and disregard it is the misfortune in life. When we know what should be done, it is our honor to do it. Not to act according to our understanding is to disregard our intelligence.

Today: If I know what ought to be done but don't do it, I really have a problem.

It might be physical—because I can't really take out the garbage if I have a broken back.

It might be psychological—because I don't "let my light shine" for others to see if I am so depressed I can't turn the light on.

Chances are that my problem is spiritual—that I'm not

really "turned on" to God enough to get out and do what I know I ought to do. I'm too much *heart* and not enough head at times. It's easier to be emotional (heart) than intellectual (head).

No Sweat?

We are told that success is ninety per cent perspiration and ten per cent inspiration. With air conditioning and a multitude of deodorants on the market it would seem that there is little hope of success at all.

In the age of the computer, most perspiring is mental; so we are forced into a situation of raising the percentage of inspiration required.

The fact is, inspiration is more likely to generate perspiration than is perspiration to generate inspiration. Man cannot obtain greatness without the inspiration.

The inspired athlete finds victory more easily than one who merely considers the exercise involved. He doesn't count the cost but values the prize.

The man with the idea is going further than one whose prowess is measured in muscles. The idea is a sharing in the infinite—the muscles are sadly finite.

Christ was given the strength to redeem the human race by accepting the inspiration that it was the Father's will. We are allowed to go on our stumbling, fumbling, confused way with confidence because Our Lord has told us He would send us the Holy Spirit to call to our minds whatsoever He had taught.

In the Agony of the Garden, Jesus perspired blood—but only because He was inspired by the knowledge of His Oneness with the Father. If we are a people of Faith, we too have that inspiration.

Today: To inspire or perspire—that's the question. If I'm inspired, I might end perspiring. If I'm perspiring, I might inspire others. So, there's a vicious circle. It just might be that someday I'll sweat blood—in pain, in agony, in death!!

Dear God, don't let me make a fool of myself when I am in my last agony. Keep me united to you and your will and when I start to shake, or vomit, or groan, let me do it alone. But if my friends are standing around, let them remember some good in me and pray for me for the evil I've done.

God is Love

Before marriage, the couple spends a great deal of time impressing one another that one is not worthy of the other. And in a healthy marriage, the situation continues. As soon as the man thinks he is good enough for his wife, he has ceased loving her.

Love is life. Either it continuously grows or it is dead. The greater effort put forth to prove love, the more the realization of failure and shortcomings of oneself.

Love demands a togetherness. There comes a time when one quits asking whether he is worthy of his spouse and begins to use the words "we" and "us" and "ours" instead of "you and I" and "yours and mine."

It is no longer a situation of being worthy, but rather of being "one." Love demands a unity—of mind, heart, and affections. A person cannot say his thoughts and actions are unworthy of his partner, because both share the thoughts and actions.

There must be a constant search in which each reads and understands the other—not with the idea of eliminating surprises, but rather to constantly be surprised with the depth of richness found in growing together.

It used to amaze me how married people eventually begin to look alike—especially when one compares their vast differences at the time of marriage. How important it is to be "one."

Isn't it impressing that Christ wants us all to be "one in Him" just as He is "one with the Father"? To be joined together in Christ is the ultimate "we."

Today: What a thought—Jesus and I make a WE!!! If I realize that, life doesn't seem so bad. I never live alone, for Jesus is with me!!

In fact, Jesus is the better part of WE. I'm the "scrub"—the "shrimp." Life can be great when I don't go it alone, but death—that's different. In death I'll go it alone, unless I make sure that Jesus is still with me. My faith tells me, "He'll be there."

Generation Gap

Somehow, we have been convinced that this century is experiencing the first real "generation gap." Somehow, too, we are convinced that the generation gap can happen only when there are hippies or yippies or squares—where there is not only a lack of communication, but also a refusal to communicate.

The fact is, the New Testament talks about a generation gap in the life of Christ. He was only twelve at the time and quite "lost" as far as His parents were concerned—even though He was lost in the temple.

It wasn't a case of disobedience or insolence—it was a matter of misunderstanding—on Mary and Joseph's part. When they found Him, they were upset and let Him know in quite specific terms.

His response, as a response of a twelve year old's can be, was totally disarming: "Did you not know I must be about my Father's business?"

The young, today, are often convinced they have more important things to do than follow the designs of their parents. Sometimes it is for the good of society; sometimes for the cause of nation, the world or God—almost as though the parents are against such causes.

Many times parents might do well to follow Mary's honest example—to admit she did not comprehend a word He had spoken. Sometimes if parents would listen they might understand the spirit and charity of their children. And sometimes with the parent's confidence, as with Christ, the next generation could "grow in wisdom, knowledge and grace before God and man."

Today: Gaps are empty spaces—gaps imply there is a distance between. It might be an empty space causing a broken exhaust pipe, a leak in a gas line, a canyon between mountains or a misunderstanding between people. Any misunderstanding is unfortunate but when it is between parents and children, it is worse.

When one stands beside an empty grave and watches a coffin being lowered, it might be rather late to "fix up" a generation gap—so do it TODAY.

"Go Teach!"

Annually, the editorial page and letters to the editor discuss teachers' salaries. The letters invariably miss some very human, but obvious, realities. So often I hear parents saying such things as the following: "If we have one more snow day, I'm going to lose my mind." or "You can't imagine what a relief it is when the house gets quiet on Monday morning when the children are at school."

Instead of flopping in the state of utter exhaustion after a hectic weekend with the children, it might be well to write each of your children's teachers a letter of deep gratitude (and perhaps a copy of one to the local editor) and praise the teacher for doing such a marvelous task with twenty to forty or so of children just like yours, for five days of the week.

If the teacher did nothing but baby-sit, he or she would be earning every cent paid. The teacher is responsible for every personality and character trait the child needs to develop where the parent may have failed. And if the teacher fails, he or she is much more likely to hear about that during the next Parent-Teacher Conference than to receive any praise for his or her innumerable successes.

And before space runs out in this article, it may be well to mention that the educational tools required for the essentials of life for the next generation of breadwinners are adequately provided in the classroom—or else.

God bless our teachers whose lives are always under the community microscope, who daily have the courage to face martyrdom in the name of truth, and who once a year ask for raises so they aren't totally ignored by the American population.

Today: "Go teach" are two words directly from the lips of Jesus Christ, but what a challenge!

Jesus also invites us to "Come and see." Between the *Come* and the *Go*, there is time for growth, change and conversion.

Teachers sometimes like to say of their former students, "I helped make him what he is _____!" That's right, teachers do make indelible marks on children—parents do too. At the age of _____ I'm still carrying around some indelible marks made by my teachers in that brick school house on the hill. God bless those who "go and teach" in the name of Jesus. Parents, that includes you.

"Suffer the Little Children"

Shortly after the Nixon election, a mother and father were discussing what changes might take place under the new administration. Their first grader listened intently and eventually spoke her piece: "I don't care what else he does as long as he doesn't make us go to school every day."

For utilization of space and saving the taxpayer, perhaps the school should be open twelve months of the year, but I think Bridget, the first grader, was being realistic.

If we want computers to teach, fine. If we want human beings as teachers, they need to get away from it all once in a while too. The Church teaches that the parents have the primary obligation of educating the child. At present the child doesn't see either parent for nine months of the year—and those are the nine months when the child is underfoot, hardly allowed outside. The teacher needs a rest not only for his good, but more importantly for the good of the child.

Today, our educational system demands an ever improving situation for the child. More and more pressures are placed on the teacher for higher degree work and intensive workshops. Some of these can be accomplished by attending night school (after teaching all day) provided one teaches close enough to a college. Otherwise, the summer months are important for refresher courses and further studies.

For many teachers, it is a twelve-month-a-year job; nine months on one side of the desk teaching; and three months on the other side, learning. And you know, those three months are fairly expensive!

Today: The child is the important factor in the teaching-learning component. I pray for those students whose teachers have become like computers—no mess, no fuss!! You just push and punch and away it goes! Out comes a finished product. 'Tis so unlike "what a wonderful piece of work is man." Teachers, refresh yourselves!!

Dedication

For the past two weeks, the articles have been on teachers and salaries. Here we go once more. In a letter to the editor on this question, a point was made that ministers are just as dedicated as teachers and receive much less in material gain. I suppose the fact could be disputed, but here I'm more interested in someone who teaches, is dedicated and receives much less than anyone—the Catholic nun or sister.

I once heard a prominent lay theologian say we should close all Catholic high schools because the students at that age are generally apathetic and why should we have them hating the sisters.

That was a few years ago, when parents and children alike showed a complete and deserved respect for the religious. The sisters are just as dedicated as ever. They, because of vocation shortage and greater educational demands, are working harder than ever. The mystery is— Why don't people continue showing respect for this dedication?

Karl Marx says everything depends on economics. We hate to give him credit for anything, but maybe he is right in this situation. Too many Catholics have begun to look upon the school sisters as just so much cheap help—not as fools for the sake of Christ, but just fools.

The "good old days" when everyone had at least one favorite nun and parents constantly showed signs of appreciation for the sisters are gone. The sister is taken for granted and given less attention than the locks on the school doors. No one, not even a dedicated sister, can survive under such inconsideration.

If we each had a "bit" more dedication to education, we would show more respect to our sisters, we would put a "bit" more in the collection basket to pay our lay faculty in Catholic schools a living wage, and we would rejoice that the public school teacher, in demanding higher wages, is constantly bringing before all of us the fact that every worthy teacher is a dedicated person worthy of his pay!

Today: Wow!! Seems "Father" is a little protective of the "good sisters!" But then—he has his reasons. My dad used to say that you get just as much respect in life as you deserve. Maybe that goes for the "good" sisters too.

More power to the sister who is taken for granted. If

she is really a "religious" sister she will use this as just one more opportunity to be like her Spouse, Jesus—the most abject of men.

Thanks for the sympathy though, dear, dear Father.

The Thaw

A college counsellor recently stated that discouragement is more serious and difficult to combat with one who suffers from depression when the spring thaw cuts through the winter's long nights and cold days.

When all about them feel the heavy load of snow weighing hard upon them, and when they speak words of great discontent concerning the harsh winter, the depressed feel normal and ordinary and assume they are, as all society, quite normal in their reactions.

But on the sunny day, when all about them begins to rejoice in warmth, the naturally depressed person allows his spirits to sink even lower because he is no longer a part of the society about him.

The very sun which gladdens some men's hearts is the source of sadness for another. And so it is with all of the things of Nature about us.

Realizing this, each one of us, whether we live in joy or sadness, must not do so to the extent that others' feelings may be forgotten. And those who are misunderstood, should try to recognize the situation as it is: that we are misunderstood because of a lack of understanding, rather than from another's meanness.

And whether we rejoice or become depressed by the advent of "good" weather, let us who rejoice show understanding and love to others—and let those of us who may be depressed accept the love.

Where Nature fails to give all men satisfaction—love provides. And each of us can know and appreciate God's mercy only as it is translated, given and accepted by man.

Today: Some years the winter thaw comes in March or April— but it is also known to have come only in May. I just better not depend on the spring thaw to warm my heart. A real physicist would say that it *takes heat* from the atmosphere to thaw the ice. Logically, that leaves even less heat.

I hereby resolve not to depend on the coming and going

of the sun for my good days nor my bad days, for my love and joy.

The love in my heart cannot and will not depend on the winter thaw!! God forbid.

"I Know Mine"

One hears it all too often: "People go to Communion just because everybody else is doing it" or "Communion doesn't do much for me, I must lack faith. I don't even think holy things when I receive."

Isn't it a shame that people can be upset by such utterances and concepts. If we are truly a Community of Christians, then it is essential that we act both as a Community and as Christians—and what better and explicit way than being one in Christ.

To complain about distractions while receiving Christ is to regulate Christ from your total existence. He does not want to enter our thoughts only when He enters our bodies.

It is much more logical and theological that we bring our entire persons to be united in Christ. This means our temptation, our "distractions," our plans for the family, our problems, our sadness, our joys should be proper subjects for consideration when we communicate.

To communicate only thoughts of Christ when we receive is, in a sense, not allowing Christ to communicate with us—but a somewhat phony momentary "us" which will cease to exist when we leave the church.

What a tragedy it would be to commune without communicating oneself! Or to forget that in Communion we are part of a Community dedicated to Christ.

Today: Communion! Holy Communion! First Communion! These are all such familiar terms, but so is Jesus familiar to me. Communion and Jesus are two words that go together. Someday I will be in communion with Him forever. Before then I must suffer a little more, pray a little more and maybe even work a little more.

Jesus, someday I want to be united with you in a very special way, FOREVER. I know I'll never make it alone. Without you, Jesus, I can do nothing. Help! Help! Help!

He is Risen

St. Paul writes that if Christ has not risen from the grave, then our faith is in vain. The Apostle is stressing the concept of faith in Christ's divinity. It is particularly easy, on Easter Sunday, to forget the humanity of Christ. Yet, Our Lord wants us to have faith in Him as man also.

Much emphasis is placed on His manhood in the Easter narratives. Mary Magdalen mistakes Christ for a gardener when she asks, "Where have you placed Him?"

The disciples on the road to Emmaus fail to recognize Him during a lengthy conversation and journey—"until the breaking of the bread."

Thomas, the doubting Apostle, demands physical evidence that the risen Savior is indeed the Christ, when he protests he will not believe until he can put his fingers into the wounds of the hands and his hands into the gaping opening in the flesh of Christ.

When the Apostles come to the shore after a night of fishing, they recognize the Messiah as He prepares a meal for them and He eats with them.

For forty days Christ teaches as one with authority—no longer in parables, but plainly. During this time, even though He was risen from the dead, He displayed His humanity.

Let us not forget the two-fold faith demanded of Christians by the Easter message: Christ is God; Christ is man. To deny either is to be less than a complete believer in the Incarnation and the message of the cross.

Today: A fancy way of saying what Father is talking about is to say that God is both transcendental and immanent. So my faith must lead "up" and "over," God is "in heaven" and "in the world." To exclude either is to limit the greatness of God. Just as surely as my thoughts go *up* to God, so they must go out and *over* to my neighbor.

Some days it is easier to please only God, but then on other days I don't find human beings so bad. Dear Lord, make my heart all inclusive. Keep me from being exclusive, even exclusively for God. To God, through my neighbor is my motto!!

"Body of Christ"

When most of us receive the Eucharist, we are impressed from our early training that we are being made one with God. We forget, somehow, that we are partaking of the Body, Blood, Soul and Divinity of Christ.

St. Paul tells us that in the Passion of Christ He became sin for us. Generally this is interpreted as meaning He took upon Himself all the results of sin upon all of mankind. The consequences of such suffering is beyond our finite minds.

When we contemplate the shock and sense of loss from the murder of one of our leaders—and realize as far as God is concerned, one man is as important as another—then we might begin to realize what the Passion involved just for the sins of murder since the beginning of time.

Add to that the resulting suffering from the breaking of the rest of the Commandments and we know that Our Lord becoming sin is incomprehensible.

Just as He became sin—and thereby rejected by all at Calvary—so at Communion He comes to us, not as sin, but one who has conquered sin. He comes representing all the virtues known to mankind. He comes representing a joining of all the virtuous men from the first man until the end of time.

The Eucharist is a joining together then, of the present Christian Community, not only with one another, but more importantly with all men of love who have ever lived or will ever live.

With this concept in mind, it is easy to see why the Scripture insists that we must make all things right with our neighbors before approaching the altar, since we are about to receive our brother, in the flesh, who represents and indeed is the entire Community of the people of God.

When we say "Amen" we are acknowledging our part in the Community of the Faithful. We say "Amen" to the fact that we are joined physically and spiritually in Him.

Today: I'm only one member of the Body of Christ! What a dejecting thought. I'd like to think that I'm the whole thing—all by myself. That would make me the VITAL statistics. As it is, I'm only a member. I can be a squeaking member or an aching member. I could also be a vibrant, alive, energetic member.

Member plus member plus member equals a WHOLE. Many members make one body, just as many Christians make one Christian Community. In the *old* math or the *new* math the sum of parts equal wholes.

Anyway, Lord, help me with my spiritual math.

To Belong

Most of us can look back on our childhood with one memory in common—the recollection of being sent to bed without eating. This was considered an excellent means of punishment.

At the next meal, one was hesitant as to whether or not he should be seated at his regular place at table. It was always a welcome relief when the food was passed around and you were included.

The great punishment was not necessarily missing the meal. In fact, there was a possibility you were being punished for complaining about the food. The real punishment rested in the fact that you were no longer accepted as a member of the family. You suddenly realized you weren't a part of the community which shared a common roof.

The Eucharist, in our lives, is the food given us by the Son of God at the Last Supper. When one is not worthy to eat His flesh and drink His blood, he writes himself off as a member, in good standing, of the Christian community.

But, just as one, as a child, returns to the family table as an act of reconciliation, so also is it the case with a person when he receives the Eucharist.

He is sharing the banquet of the Lord with the community, which is the people of God. Isn't it interesting that as children we were always anxious to return to the table—yet so many miss the opportunity of being one in Christ as He is one with the Father—to be part of the community established in the love from the cross!

Today: Either I belong or I don't belong—I'm either *in* or *out* of the Christian community. Receiving Jesus in the Eucharist is based on the assumption that I'm in His circle. As a child playing "drop the handkerchief," I was always glad to again hold hands with those in the circle.

So the comparisons go—but there's a possibility that I might miss the whole point. I must strive daily to make myself a worthy member of Christ's family, or I may just be the one to become the black sheep.

Such a job—being good in life and in death.

E Pluribus Unum

This Latin phrase, found on many forms of American money, means "One from many." From time to time there have been discussions to remove this slogan, or at least put it in English. For some reason, the government is unwilling to give up the Latin.

Whether it be in English or Latin, the idea is good. No one wants to be alone all the time—and there are times when being alone is particularly hard.

Perhaps because of our early discipline, it is particularly difficult to eat alone. It is always hard for the child to be told he must take his plate, leave the table and eat by himself in some remote area in or out of the house.

A widower develops irregular eating habits because he does not want to eat alone. The widow, even though she may be an excellent cook through years of experience in feeding her husband and family, suddenly loses all interest in cooking because it isn't worth the effort when one has to eat alone.

There is one moment in each day when Christ beckons us—when He tells us to share the Banquet with the Community of Christians. That moment, of course, takes place in the Mass when many people from all walks of life join together in Him, with Him and through Him—*E Pluribus Unum*. We are the many; He is the One!

Today: I'm not particularly interested in reviewing my Latin, but I guess the concept of E Pluribus Unum could be reviewed.

The geometry axiom states that the whole is equal to, but not greater than its parts. It must be the same way with us—with people. This nation, although it may stand under God, is not greater than, but equal to its parts.

Today I will examine myself as a part of the whole. I pray I won't be like that one last part of a jigsaw puzzle that is missing at the end, but that I'll be *one* of the *many* parts, all fitting together.

Christ, Not the Sky, is the Limit

Since the "Apollo 8" moonshot, there has been much discussion as to whether or not it was really worth it. The question is heard again and again: "With so many Americans living in poverty, couldn't we have spent the money more wisely?"

Several years ago scientists told the world the trip around the moon was possible. All that was needed was enough money. After it was all over, they actually showed some concern that the one hundred and forty-seven hour flight ended twenty seconds over time. It seems there must be an obvious conclusion—the scientists knew what they were doing.

The same cannot be said about solving the problems of the slums and the ghettos. No one has come up with the answers—no one has provided a master plan whereby he can say it will take so long and so many dollars. The dealing isn't with test tubes, silos and rockets, it is with human beings.

In most instances, these persons have never been able to place faith in anyone or anything. No one has gone out of his way to prove love, but generally to save conscience. There is no reason for those in slums to have hope.

A little child learns to walk because a loving mother directs and exhorts him to walk to a loving father. In the simple process of walking, he inherits faith, hope and love. He can always fall back on these precious moments in time of doubt. The person in the ghetto has few, if any, precious moments to recall.

Somehow, each one of us must turn, not to government funds, but the "Sermon on the Mount" in St. Matthew. If each of us could live the words of Christ found there, the solution would be realized.

Unfortunately, it is easier to pay taxes and rejoice in moon flights, than to follow the exacting requirements of being a follower of Christ.

Today: Is it impossible, difficult or easy to be a follower of Christ? It might depend upon how closely, how exactly one follows. Then there's that Sermon on the Mount. That really puts demands on a person. You've got to be poor in spirit, humble, patient, meek, and besides that you are supposed to thirst for hunger and justice. No wonder I don't have time to work in the slums and ghetto areas.

Jesus just demands so much. Some day He may ask for my life besides. Wow!! I guess for now, I'll just trust Him.

Mother's Day

Nearly everyone has heard the song or poem entitled "Mother"— the one that starts out with "M is for the million things she told me." The rest of the words are a deep tribute to all deserving mothers.

Sometimes, it seems to children that the first line is quite accurate— but the words for them continue differently:
"O is for the other things she told me"
"T is for the thousands of things she told me"
"H is for the hundreds of things she told me"
"E is for everything else she told me"
"R is for the rest of what she told me."

The fact is that such a mother should be saluted as much as the one for whom the original words were intended. A true mother who sincerely loves her children is going to tell them everything she knows which will benefit them in any way.

It may be that some things she says are unimportant and irrelevant, but when spoken, the intention is not so. She wants to speak and teach love.

Unfortunately, it isn't until the child is no longer a child that the things which mother said all become important and meaningful.

What a shame that so often a mother's love is not appreciated until it is no more. Then is when the person can say, "I wish she had said more things to me, and I wish I had been more mindful."

Today: It is hard to stand by and watch your mother's coffin slowly go down, down!! And then there's that clump of dirt you hear as it hits the top. People walk away and you just know it's all over. You'll never see mom again. It's then you start living with your "if only I . . . " Each human being has *one* and only one mother. Because there is only one, it is better not to hurt the one you have.

Listen, all of you who still have your mother alive— "there just ain't no one like her." Imprint her words on your heart now. Glory be to all mothers.

"Togetherness"

No matter how good the food might be, it loses its savor if someone you love cannot share with you. It is difficult to enjoy a thick, juicy steak in the dining room if your spouse, parent or child has the flu and cannot eat at all.

In Christian terms, this can be translated into receiving the Eucharist when we know there are devout Christians in a part of the world where "no-priest land" is law.

It means accepting the body and blood of Christ with the knowledge that others are not doing so because they lack faith.

It is to live in the ultimate luxury of absolute Communion with God while another exists within the solitary loneliness of self.

There is a time in life, when we are little children, when one is expected to say, "This is mine." When we grow up, this phrase becomes more distasteful to oneself and to others.

A person in love with another wants to say and hear, "This is ours." The adult Christian must move away from the concept, even at Communion, of Jesus and I. We must learn the reality of Jesus and Us. He did not die for me alone. I cannot totally rejoice in being one with Christ as long as someone else is not.

Today: "Togetherness" is a funny word especially in this age of personalism. I want to be me—I want to do my thing. Doing "our" thing—being communal—and respecting everyone else's feelings and likes is difficult.

Maybe if I think about it some more, pray about it and receive Christ more reverently it'll become easier.

What's all this holding hands at the Our Father, or shaking hands and calling it a kiss of peace all about?

Individual—personal—alone—ah me!!

Come, Holy Spirit

Before and after each class, the School Sisters of Notre Dame, novices and postulants take turns leading a short, meaningful prayer. Once in a while they sing. Sometimes they sing in unison; sometimes they harmonize. When they sing in unison, it is good; when they harmonize, it is magnificent.

A single tree is indeed a beautiful thing. It can be more or less so according to the season. But it is a rare tree that is more beautiful by itself than when it blends with others in a landscape or a mountainside.

Many of the animals are able to blend into the background Nature provides them for protection. Some even change colors according to the season to perfect the camouflage.

The plan of God is that all of Nature live in a harmony. The Scripture tells us that the divine plan calls for the filling of the valleys and the leveling of the hills. Scripture allows the lamb and the lion a happy companionship.

Man, without God, destroys the balance and the harmony—not only in Nature, but more especially amongst mankind itself.

Pentecost is the moment in history which advertises to all that man with God shares in one harmonious whole. He does not give up his individuality any more than the singer or the tree, but he does give his individual gifts for a more perfect response to the demands of Christ—and consequently takes his place in the total picture of redemption drawn by Our Savior.

Today the Tower of Babel situation is reversed. Men torn apart by pride so they can no longer communicate are now brought together in spite of many tongues, in an understanding through the love of the Spirit.

Today: Maybe Scripture allows a lion and a lamb a happy companionship, but what about North and South Vietnam? What about East and West Germany? Then there is husband and wife? Neighbor? Living without destroying harmony isn't all it seems to be. It's just too hard some days. Some days I need the "dove" of Pentecost to land on my head to help me over the hump. When nothing

else brings peace I can still say, Come, Holy Ghost.
Maybe the Tower of Babel in me will be reversed yet.

Freedom?

Americans have been sold for so long on independence that they have sometimes forgotten its real meaning. One cigarette company actually tells us that independent thinkers are dependent on its product!

We train our young people with such an attitude of independence as a virtue that they are afraid to be dependent, even on God.

The point we so easily miss is that dependence is one of life's essentials. Young lovers, at any age, will go to any extent to prove their need for one another—that they desire dependence on one another for the rest of their lives.

But, they are so determined to live in independence that they are anxious to prove they are finally without need of parental help or advice. Love becomes a liberation from former dependence rather than a deep gratitude for a new love—a new dependence.

We all want independence from tyranny of any kind—but love is not a tyranny, it is an absolute essential to life. Let us all pray that we may remain independent, that in freedom we might choose the wonderful dependence—or inter-dependence on one another—in Christ.

As Christians let us be grateful for the independence which has been our trademark, but let us pray, too, that our lives might be filled with the wonderful dependence allowed men of free will!

Today: Who is independent? I think we're all slaves in one way or another; slaves to tobacco, drugs, speed on the highway or sports on T.V. There are some things I am no longer able to do for myself—I'm too dependent. Today I'll do as I please—I'll pray an extra hour, read a book, take a hike and eat raw carrots.

Thanks, God, for the spirit of independence in this good old U.S.A. I don't know what I'd do without it.

99 44/100% is Not Good Enough

Starvation is a terrible thing. It is slow, it is painful, it is ugly. Newspapers show us pictures of starving people throughout the world. Many authors, such as Dickens, play on our heartstrings with such unfortunates as Tiny Tim. Bodily starvation is terrible.

We have all seen pictures of a street urchin looking hauntingly into a bakery window with wistful eyes and drawn face. Compassion immediately springs into our mind and heart.

As adults, we can remember in our childhood that there were always kind people giving us candy, cookies, or cake. We appreciated them and were sorely disappointed when a favorite friend in the neighborhood would be away and it would do no good to walk slowly back and forth in front of his or her house awaiting the good news of a treat.

I really feel sorry for children today who must forsake the possibility of such generous charity. They are not allowed to fully participate in what should and could be a true community. But, I really feel sorry for the adults who want so much to give candy, ice cream, and cake to little children because they love little children so very much and they cannot share. To give to a child out of genuine love and be suspected is tragic. To give to a child out of a desire to be generous and allow the child to be tricked by the next person is even more tragic.

Somehow, parents, tell your children, and indeed you must, that they must never accept anything from anyone unless you are with them. Go ahead. Tell them that some people cannot be trusted—but tell them, too, that the majority of us are "starving" to share everything we could with them and are really sad that we cannot.

Sooner or later, they must find out anyway, that it only takes an absolute minority to spoil many of the truly great things in life for the majority.

Today: An absolute minority could be one person. If it takes only one to spoil a good thing then obviously it only takes one person to do a good thing. One person with conviction and dedication is worth 99 standing around criticizing and complaining. Dear God, don't let me follow the mob!! Let me act with zeal, even when I'm the only one. Incidentally, I can identify with those who "starve" to share everything yet just never get around to it.

Relax, Dad, it's Sunday,

Father's Day is always so embarrassing. We all love Dad so very much—and we really want to give him the very best at the grand time set aside for him. But the situation always presents such a conundrum. He can't afford all we would like to do for him—and even if he could, it's embarrassing to ask for that much money.

Besides, one really can't improve Dad's situation. It isn't that everything is that wonderful, but he is a hard man to change. It doesn't make much sense to spend thirty-five dollars on a new hat because the old one has at least eleven good years in it—and the antique slippers cannot be matched in comfort (and, unfortunately, in appearance).

He could use a grass trimmer, but that is too obviously a hint that there are quite a few unfinished tasks in the yard—and, after all, this is his day! Better to buy the trimmer for Christmas—maybe a snow shovel for Father's Day, if it weren't so incongruous.

In his less sane moments, he has hinted rather strongly for a bench saw, but that is just a passing fancy and he is too clumsy to work with anything so risky—and we would have to dismantle the ping pong table where we keep the yarn and life jackets and that sort of thing.

There must be something special to do for Dad. Something novel and different that would surprise and please him. Is it possible that we are missing something obvious and simple he would appreciate?

He deserves the best. "Dad, you are the greatest. We love you. Our prayers today are all for you." If his heart can take that, he may even want to be around again next year.

And go ahead, Mom, buy a new hat for the occasion. Nothing makes Dad feel better than seeing you happy and he, as we said, deserves happiness!

Today: 'Tis Father's Day again! It comes around once each year. I wonder how come we can't do it up once and for all—why show Dad thanks and appreciation little by little, piece by piece, year after year.

Why do so many people neglect really showing Dad how much he means until he is sick, old, or even dead?

Everyone has only one *Dad*—the best Dad. Why is it so embarrassing to tell him so? Someday it will be too late to tell him so.

No Defense, Please!

There are some moments in life which are automatically times of love because they are times of sharing. Two of these are found in the act of eating and the act of married love.

It is a tradition in nearly every age and area that one put aside all weapons when one engages in eating. The words *host* and *guest* have a semi-sacred connotation. They are words indicating friendship. It is quite a contradiction of terms to refer to an unwanted host—and an unwanted guest is really not a guest at all.

In marriage, too, there is a complete openness to one another. Both allow themselves to be totally defenseless. One cannot give totally and be defensive at the same time. There is demanded in marriage a sharing of mind, heart and bodies.

The Eucharist was instituted by Christ in such a manner that it allows both concepts. He comes to us as food. He is literally our Host—and, as with the Apostles on Holy Thursday, we are His guests.

Further, He demands that we become one with Him in mind, heart and body. We share His entire being. We receive His body, blood, soul and divinity.

These moments of love between God and man are limited only by man. Christ allows Himself to be without defense. Christ requested a regular and an oft-repeated Communion. "As often as you do it." Let us make and keep all things right with our neighbors, so we can be prepared for our oneness with Christ.

Today: Defense! Defensive! Defenseless! Three interesting words. Each one says so much. Just now I am curious about why people are so defensive at times. When one is most defenseless, one is most truly dependent on God. At the moment of my death I will be truly defenseless. Then, hopefully, I will say, "Thy will be done."

At that moment, I will have nothing "of me" to defend.

In the act of eating, loving, receiving Jesus in Communion and in the moment of dying, my best and only defense is my undying trust and faith. May it grow stronger each day, especially today.

For Better or for Worse

All day long, nearly every working day, man puts on his mask and ventures into the world of business—and business decrees that the mask reflect joy and happiness, assurance and equanimity.

The teacher smiles at the principal, cajoles the students to greater heights of educational interest, exchanges pleasantries with fellow faculty, is charming with the custodian—all through headache number two hundred and four.

The banker grins a pleasant refusal to a bad risk. He praises the cashier for industriousness. He emotes enthusiasm with the bank examiner—he promotes confidence in the investor—despite the fact his headache is number sixty-seven.

The waitress hastens to wait on the undesirable hungry monster in booth three with a pleasant "Good morning, sir, would you like a menu?" Her charm fills the room when she asks with deep interest whether everything is all right even when she knows that Venus de Milo is more likely to leave a tip. Joyfully, she cleans up the mess caused when a beautiful, unwatched child tips the Chef's special onto the floor. Headache number _____.

At quitting time, the masks come off. All the way home, the smiles melt and aching bones seek respite in a favorite chair. Home, sweet home! Where everyone is allowed the grand privilege of being his own ugly self and be loved in spite of it.

All the frustrations of the day, for those working out of the house or those staying behind to clean, cook or what have you, are brought out magnificently by an entire family of inconsiderate individuals. Somehow, everyone understands and accepts the situation as it is. There is a genuine relationship where all see through the foibles of the others—and there is love!

Today: Most people hate facades. We dislike masks, yet I wonder if we could stand life, even for one day, if people didn't wear masks.

If teachers didn't smile through two hundred and four headaches, what then? If bankers didn't grin a pleasant refusal, what then? If waitresses didn't clean up the mess after headache number _____. So, the list goes on and on—everybody "acting" the part—the image! What would one day be like if no one play acted—if no one wore a mask. Maybe tonight I'll thank God for masks. Life might be worse, just maybe.

"Taps?"

In recent times the American flag has been desecrated, not only abroad, but right in the United States. Many times this has been done by enemies, sometimes by friends, who really think they are doing the world a favor.

This, in itself, is alarming enough to most of us, but even more so is the waving of Communist flags. Even more alarming to some is the fact that some are not alarmed.

The answer given by some people who care little for the American, is they prefer to think in terms of the brotherhood of man rather than the superiority of any country. I think all of us want to have a brotherhood.

Today, America is the leading power in the world. Whether she deserves to be so is disputed. Those who want her to relinquish this power should at least acknowledge that at present only two other nations are likely to succeed to the world power: Red China or Communist Russia.

No one should pretend that all is right with and in America. It isn't. One need not list the litany of problems facing us—many of them are self evident. A cursory perusal of the newspapers is proof enough. And it isn't any good to answer all problems with the statement, "Things could be worse." Indeed, they are worse elsewhere.

For over fifty years Communism had been the governing force in Russia. Great strides forward have taken place, but where isn't this the case over the same period of time. Not many Americans would want things as they were fifty years ago.

It seems we are faced with two choices. The American dream with all its nightmares or the Communist nightmare with all its dreams. Let us not lower the flag too hastily.

Today: I wouldn't go so far as to say "My country, right or wrong," but I do have confidence in America.

America doesn't need to be the most powerful nation in the world, but I want it to be the most humane nation in the world.

My prayer today is that when any man is hungry, then we

are all hungry. When anyone is oppressed, we all share that oppression.

When any one of us starts to lower the flag, or starts to play "taps" for this good old U.S.A., then we are all DEAD.

Long live America.

Don't Play Dead!

A pacifier is a great help in raising children. It always helps calm the mother's nerves. Something of great interest is the fact that pacifiers can take so many forms for the young.

One of the most common is generally considered that which is merely the nipple from the baby's bottle—designed in such a way that the child cannot swallow the object.

A means of pacification which is often used for a much longer duration is the toy gun. A child, with a minimum of intelligence, quickly discovers its potential.

And there can be such variety to spice "life." Automatically, depending on the type of gun, he can be a soldier, a cowboy, a gangster, a detective, a big game hunter—or what have you! Every youngster has great imagination and little of it is required in such instances.

At all types of gatherings one might find a young lad with his pacifier. He will proceed from one person to another, pointing at a vital area such as the heart or head, and pull the trigger. Each guest in turn responds with the desired effect. He clasps his breast or head and does his utmost for the child's coveted Oscar in the throes of a pretended death struggle.

The Oscar winner is rewarded by eventually being singled out by the youngster for repeated performances, much to the glee of everyone. Reincarnation is unquestioned as long as the subject is willing to die again.

Finally, the Oscar winner grows tired of the game and stays dead. This forces the child to search out a new victim for his pacifier. New actors are found and die in turn.

When one views the dead and dying it seems almost time to take the gun from the child and ask the question, "What price pacification?"

Today: Why *play* dead when death is the truest reality of all? I haven't quite figured out yet whether death is pacifying or not. Are dead people peaceful people? If not, a pacifier won't do much good then.

Today I am going to live as I will wish I had lived everyday—peacefully! Today could even be my last day, too. One of these days my life will be over.

Have a Heart

The worst sickness that can befall a man is not cancer or anything that pertains to the physical, but rather that which is spiritual. This is a sickness which each of us has suffered in some way at some time—home sickness!

All have shared the sentiments of the little girl who, when being asked if she was homesick, quickly responded: "No, I'm here-sick."

To know there is love which you can share and yet find yourself unable to share is a very human experience. To know there is a love which you cannot share eternally is hell. Hell is eternal homesickness.

If one finds such sickness so difficult on a temporary basis, it is utter foolishness to risk it on a permanent one. Such a risk is the ultimate foolishness.

In our power to know and love, we are like unto God. To know and not to love is self deprivation. St. James, in his Epistle says the devil in hell believes and trembles. The role of the Christian is to believe and love.

The little girl's statement on "here-sickness" is something to meditate about. He who loves is not "here-sick" but "here-happy." "God is love" and not to love is to forget God.

Yet, we cannot forget the God who made us, and redeemed us—the giver of all and to all. We merely forget His love—and lose all. Let us not be fools. Let there be love.

Today: I wish I were homesick—homesick for God—homesick for heaven.

> If I were really homesick for God, then I wouldn't feel so sorry for myself when I get sick. I might even look forward to the day of my death. For me, then, death would really be going home. Oh, yes, someday I am going home—not by bus, train, plane or car but by one last grasp of breath—maybe just one *choke*!

To Move Mountains

Whether we want to admit it or not, we live in a world of faith. In our ordinary conversations, we don't respond to each statement with, "Prove it." We are accustomed to presuming truth.

If someone tells us the river is thirty feet deep, we don't go wading—at least not without water wings. If someone tells us, "That snake is poisonous," we are anxious to accept his word.

History points to the fact that humans are constantly being had. The Crusaders believed it when it was said, "God wills it." Jacob didn't know he had been tricked until he was married to the wrong woman.

There has always been a credibility gap where man just didn't know any better. The problem is that the gap exists where he does know better! Every time we watch a TV ad, we know better but we want to believe what is "possible" for us.

The American system demands faith in man. One is presumed innocent until proven guilty. Faith begets faith. If I believe you, the honor is returned. If I say, "I wish I could have faith in you," some of your faith in me is lost.

If it is sensible and for one's good that he have faith in man, it is much more logical that he have faith in God. Perhaps, this is why the acceptance of Christ has persisted nearly two thousand years despite the fact there have been so few real Christians.

Christ continues rising from the dead with each new generation which in turn does its best to crucify Him again. It is time that this generation learns to cling to faith. We have need of faith because there are mountains to be moved, vipers to be caressed and poison to be drunk. Let there be faith!

Today: To move a mountain? What a job. Some days it is bad enough trying to move an ant hill. Whether I try to move ant hills or mountains, I must believe in what I'm about to do.

Today I am going to examine my faith life. I'll try to answer three simple questions:

1) How do I know that I really believe in God?

2) How do I show my friends that I have an undying faith in them?

3) When was the last time I looked at myself in the mirror and said, "I trust you."

Respect vs. Respect

Human respect is the great killer of conscience. Such respect allows the other person to fiddle whatever tune he wishes for our dancing. Moral convictions evaporate quickly in the heat of human respect.

Human respect has for its foil the wonderful, soothing concept of compromise—and compromise pretends its own justifications.

Peter was paying little heed to human respect when he declared he was "filled with the Holy Spirit and had to preach Christ." And if Christ had been concerned about human respect, He would never have been crucified!

To resist the pressure of human respect, one faces a continuing threat of crucifixion—a threat of being joined intimately to Christ. One faces the choice, in his daily life, between two respects—human respect and self respect. The martyrs, unanimously, voted in favor of self respect. In a sense, they chose to be able to live with themselves rather than to die spiritually with others.

The maintaining of self respect demands the ability of following one's conscience. It demands the self knowledge required by both the Old and New Testament as the beginning of wisdom.

The Christian who truly knows himself realizes he is a tabernacle of Christ and a temple of the Holy Spirit. He recognizes a value he will not compromise. Even more important, he sees the same possibility of greatness in others and consequently allows them self respect by his love for them.

Human respect has no respect for humanity since there is no respect at all. Christian self respect has concern for all men—in Christ.

Today: Respect! Self respect, human respect, Christian respect, and I don't know what it is all about. I think it means that I like *me* better than I like *you*. I suppose I should like you better than I like myself, but that is hard.

Today I'll spend some time thinking about all the nice people I know. I'll sit here awhile and just "love" them. Maybe that could be called "other" respect. How's that for a new kind of respect?

Mind over Matter

It seems rather obvious that each of us in his life has found himself in circumstances not completely to his own liking. Quite often this circumstance is while in church.

Some time ago a mother was quite distracted in church by her daughter. The youngster was putting two fingers to her lips, sucking air with a vengeance, removing the fingers, and exhaling into the heights. From time to time she would reach out her hand, point a finger and suddenly drop it a couple of times.

After church, the mother reprimanded her child. "Why did you pretend you were smoking in church?" The daughter, without hesitation, answered, "I wasn't pretending I was smoking in church. I was pretending I wasn't in church at all."

It is good to have imagination. One can sit in church and redesign hats to one's own liking. He can imagine shadows being all sorts of weird things. He can guess how long the sermon is by the squirming of the neighbor's child—then measure his guess against his watch.

And even during the worst of sermons each of us can take a good thought from the priest's text, or from the Gospel or Epistle and weave one's sermon to himself.

One might discover how easy it is to preach a good sermon and gain by the thoughts. Or he might find how difficult it is and learn compassion for him who preaches. And one might, at various times, find it interesting to pretend he is in church.

Today: Maybe if we all gave sermons to ourselves, we'd be better people.

I'm going to try it right now—this empty space is for all things I have to say to myself that I can't put into print.

Omission Possible

Today there is much talk about possible schisms and new heresies in the Church. I'm rather afraid such a situation cannot come to pass in our generation. In fact, this is the disappointment of the twentieth century!

One might gasp at the idea that a Catholic priest can say he is afraid that a great heresy or schisms cannot come in his day. Please, take note! I use the word *cannot* rather than *will* not.

The tragic fact is that the vast majority of people aren't concerned enough about Christ and His teaching to even investigate them. Most are not interested enough to give a "tinker's darn" about a single Christian act, let alone eternal verities.

It demands too much honest concern about the Church for this generation to spring forth with new thoughts in theology—be they heretical or orthodox. There is an eagerness to "destroy the temple" but little tendency toward "raising it up."

At a Catholic laymen's convention recently, one man told me: "I wouldn't have believed it possible to eat, sleep, and drink religion for three days and find it so utterly wonderful and interesting.

Generally conversations, in any gathering place, do not pertain to the kingdom of heaven and all the things which can be added. Too few are making retreats, praying, participating in religious experiences or allowing thoughts of the Spirit.

Most are all too willing to say there are more interesting and vital things in daily life than religion. Oh, for the good old days, when religion meant enough to man that he was willing to pursue it untiringly— even when he might honestly come to the wrong conclusions.

Today: It wouldn't be so bad to talk about the kingdom of heaven if one could be sure that there really is a kingdom of heaven. That's the problem—how do you know it's for real?? I have a hunch there would be more retreating, praying and listening to the Spirit if one could really know for sure—without a doubt—that the kingdom was really up there someplace, like a big "pie in the sky."

But for me, that would take the challenge out of it—I like the mystery, the *maybe* of it all. Christ's word is good enough for me.

Caution: Men at Work

As children we learned that one of the results of original sin was that man must work and earn his daily bread by the sweat of his brow. Perhaps this is the reason children disappear so quickly when there is work to be done—they resent original sin and all its effects.

Maturity allows one to see work not as a necessity but a real source of human joy. It is in work one is allowed to experience the real sense of accomplishment—or failure, but in either case, a better knowledge of oneself.

The things we accomplish do not make us tired, they revitalize us. To perform the impossible allows us to set even higher goals to be hopefully realized. Success does not allow much rest.

In a sense, success is the tragic part of work. The time is bound to come, because of failure of health, lack of insight or ingenuity or what have you, when one is made painfully aware of the fact that he can never accomplish all he planned in life.

Sometimes, what is even worse, the things which took time and energy are considered useless and wasteful to an "unappreciative" world.

Work must be for unselfish reasons. A man who works for his own honor and glory is doomed to failure. A man who labors for a cause is a happy man even though the cause may fail.

In fact, that is somewhat the history of the Christian: To work for a cause, to give tirelessly, to be laughed at by the world, to die with much undone—with the faith and hope that future generations will finish the work—to live and die for love.

Today: It could just be that children resent "the sweat of their own brows" just as much as they resent original sin.

> Or maybe they can't find all those unselfish reasons to work for. It's not always a matter of "the reason" that makes work enjoyable or not. I think it is mostly a matter of liking what you do. If I don't like what I do and I can't do what I like, then I have a problem—a real serious problem. Today I'll try to solve the problem. I'll either start liking my job or I'll go and get one that I like. Just like that!!

Be You Doers of the Word

When God had finished the "work" of creation, He saw that it was good and He "rested." Some seem to have the idea that God has been resting since and man must do all that requires labor.

Depending on the persons involved, work often separates the men from the boys. The muscleman depends on brawn over brain. Brawn and bravery supposedly are somewhat synonymous.

Yet, the American Indian could wisely say, "Let white man work. Him invent it." To a certain extent this causes the hippy dilemma: To have what our civilization has to offer (at least some of it) without working to acquire it.

Karl Marx placed his great emphasis on the by-product of work, productivity. His axiom was "produce according to ability, consume according to need." At the opposite extreme is the rugged individualist who proclaims, "All work and no play makes jack!"

At any rate, man cares little for perspiration and its father, work. Be that as it may, there is something about work which is much worse than work—and that is the inability to work.

The man who is where he is because he never worked would willingly trade places with another. And after it is too late, he would happily be willing to work.

Christ left a heritage for his followers—"As the Father sent me, I now send you!" Christ came with a job to accomplish. His task for body and soul is now in the hands of each Christian. How can we "stand all day idle"?

Today: When men do the boys' work, the boys get lazy. When boys do the men's work, the men are out of a job. As Christ said, let every man accomplish his share. Christ sent everyone of us to do His will—to go teach in His name—to spread His Good News! How are you doing with your job?

"Unless the Seed Shall Die"

Life's busyness allows it—there's such a common rush,
That the picture of my ending is past imagination's brush.
Small things magnified, give credence to the lie:
My life is so important that I will never die.

A lot of friends have this world left—
Spouses, children and others bereft,
But I have things which must be done—
So I just keep facing the rising sun.

Age and I have long been friends,
Time heals my wounds, my muscle mends.
But it takes more sleep to get my rest—
Much more effort to do my best.

I refuse to die, I want to live.
Friends and enemies I forgive—
To cheat death, to end strife—
I'll cling to everlasting life.

Today: "Unless the seed shall die"—will I ever get those words through my head? Will I ever realize what it means "to die"?

> Theologians say we'll die—doctors predict just about when people will die and life tells me everyday, "people die."

> My head tells me I'm going to die someday. Maybe even soon, but my heart refuses to let it sink in where it makes the difference.

> Dear Lord—help me realize that I'm not going to live forever.

The Past is Biography

When Moses addressed the "burning bush" with the question, "Who are you?" the response was, "I am who am." By this, philosophers have generally come to the conclusion that God lives in an everlasting now—eternity.

The Book of Genesis tells us we are created in the image and likeness of God. Our own experience points up the fact that we share the now of the everlasting present quite completely.

Veterans of the first or second World War can read old letters, look at medals, acknowledge their serial number—and yet it all seems like part of someone else's life rather than their own. Moments that one would always remember have long since been forgotten.

The future is just as unreal. Each generation has taken its turn in laughing at the prophets who foretell what tomorrow may bring. And those who laugh the loudest seem most capable of accepting the predicted as commonplace once it becomes fact.

We are so accustomed to living only in the present that we feel sorry for those who are mired in the past and we waste little time or sympathy on the dreamers who look at the crystal ball when they could more easily drink deeply from the cup in their grasp.

The past is great only insofar as it makes possible a glorious present. The future is fine only when it gives us a "future now" of happiness.

God is good to allow us to share now, the present as a foreshadowing of the eternal and everlasting now of happiness.

Today: Today is a new day. One more day to write a part of my obituary is today. Did you ever think of that? Everyday is a day for writing one more sentence of your obituary.

No matter what the past—this day is going to be a good one. This day will never come again—this part of my obituary can never be done over. It's going to be a good day—a real good day.

To Health

Whenever one is found in want, it seems a natural reaction to blame the Church. Any poverty situation finds someone readily faulting Christianity.

It is good the Church has the reputation for being a refuge. It all began when the lame, the blind, the deaf, the mute—and even the dead were brought to Christ.

It would be tragic if the needy could find no compassion in the Christian community. It is also tragic that so many look upon the Church as a place for the sick of mind or body.

The role of the Church in the world demands not so much a constant turning to by the needy, but rather a constant living in by all.

In a hospital, it is presumed the doctors and nurses are healthy. In an institution for mental health, the staff is expected to be mentally balanced. In both situations, the patient or guest arrives to become as healthy in body and mind as those working therein.

So with the Church, the Christian must be happy and humble, filled with faith, hope, and charity that those coming to know Christ might discover him easily within the community.

The Church is much more than Lourdes or Fatima. The Church is much more than miracles and healings. The Church is the people of God who are dedicated to living Christ's principles in the home and the market place every day of the week.

Unless the Church remains healthy, there is little hope left for a sick world reaching for truth and love.

Today: That last sentence is a thought-provoking one, but I really think it needs qualifying. I presume it means that unless each one of us within the Church remains *spiritually* healthy, then the sick would get sicker yet. Maybe I just better take a day off for a spiritual inventory. There are a couple of questions I want to ask myself. Just when was the last time you prayed for those who persecute you? How long has it been since you fasted? When have you turned the other cheek? There's so much to do yet!

Self Discipline

With the relaxing or removal of many of the disciplinary laws of the Church, it is only natural that many people are bound to ask questions.

Disciplinary laws have never, or at least should never have had, the importance of teachings of the Church. These laws have sprung from the people rather than from the hierarchy. In the early Church, the Christians, aware that Christ sacrificed his flesh for them, willingly abstained from flesh on Friday—the day of His death.

The Acts of the Apostles tells us that the followers of the way gathered on the "first" day of the week rather than the seventh, a sabbath, to celebrate the Lord's Supper. Gradually the first day became accepted by Christians as the day to keep holy.

Once a custom was in effect for one hundred years, it had the effect of a law, a disciplinary law. By the same token, once a custom is rejected for the same period the law is abrogated. As the first day became the day, the seventh was no longer kept.

So also, once members of the Church had complained rather consistently, "It's Friday," the law of abstinence was reconsidered.

It is easy to arrive at two different points of view. First, we are becoming too lax and doing nothing as Christians to show our love for Christ; or second, we are maturing rapidly as Christians and are more capable of adult decisions concerning our relationship with the Lord.

At any rate, as laws become relaxed, it is well for us to be aware of the fact that unless one is careful, it is very easy to become a lax adult.

Today: The Acts of the Apostles also tells us that the early Christians shared all things in common. Guess that custom went out of practice more than 100 years ago. Ever since I can remember it's been a dog-eat-dog world. If you, you, you and me all try hard enough we can reverse that trend. All those in favor, get started now!! Let's go back to the good old days when, like the early disciples, people shared all things in common. Come to think of it, I'm going to find it rather difficult. I'll try though.

Be-Attitude

It makes little difference whether one is president, a parent, an accountant, a farmer, a banker, a lawyer, or priest. The important thing is not the position one has in life, but how well he fills it.

As one author recently wrote, "The important thing in life is not one's position, but his disposition." Years spent in medical school are of little avail if the patient refuses to come for help because the doctor lacks any personality.

The greatest lawyer in the world is what he is because people have placed confidence in him. His position is the result of his disposition toward others.

In the story of Martha and Mary, Christ declared that Mary had chosen the good part. Most of us feel that Martha was slighted on this occasion because she was working so hard while Mary relaxed.

Immediately, we make our judgment according to the position of the two. Mary is at the feet of Christ. Martha is busy in the kitchen.

Christ's decision is not according to where either is, but rather each one's disposition. No matter how hard Martha was working—no matter what she was accomplishing, it was of little importance to Christ if her attitude was wrong.

The fact is that Mary's position at the feet of Christ was much better than Martha's disposition as she prepared the necessary food.

Today: It's been a long time since I really thought about my disposition. I might even be very ugly and not even know it. Guess I'll take out some time today and get into Mary's position—right at the feet of Jesus—and think about my disposition. How about you? How's your disposition been lately? I'll pray that you aren't ugly—not even a little ugly. If you're not ugly and I'm not ugly, that makes two of us.

Remember Whom?

This is an age of the non-hero. No one expects the spectacular of the individual in our computer world. Team efforts are the rule whether one be referring to a sporting event or a landing on the moon.

Even match-making is by machine rather than by moonlight. Very little is left to the individual heart and mind. The person, in spite of efforts to the contrary, is more and more being lost.

The few heroes this decade has provided have either been destroyed in their prime—or destroyed themselves by shortcomings or mistakes.

Do we have to give up heroes in favor of machines? Is our educational system turning out only the mediocre? Are moments of greatness for the individual a thing of the past? And if so—should we rejoice or be sad?

Perhaps the real answers are impossible because all the questions are wrong. It is no longer possible to have war heroes when war has become unpopular. It is difficult having political greats when the politicians who share the limelight are often dishonest. Great writers have given way to writers who are after a fast dollar—the value of the book is not in the moral contained so much as the content of the financial contract.

The fact is that heroes will always be determined according to moral character rather than anything else. And this judgment can be made with but one comparison in mind—a comparison with Christ!

The only hero of the crusades was a non-combatant named Francis of Assisi. Martin Luther King's greatest moment was, as was the case with Christ, in his death. The final test of the hero is Christ.

Today: If this is the age of the non-hero, then what is all the competition about? I thought people compete to become heroes. If the educational system is turning out the mediocre, then where do all the "smart" guys come from? I don't think moments of greatness are things of the past. I believe that every man has his own moment of greatness. The problem is that most of us can't recognize it when it comes. Most of us miss our own "greatest moment" in life. Good grief, how blind can we get?

Air Pollution

"You know what I like about working here most?" queried the young man. "We are never allowed to curse." It sounded especially strange coming from him because his heavy cursing dated back to his early childhood. Now he wanted never to use God's name in vain, again.

It may be very embarrassing to speak out to a friend when he uses an expletive involving our Creator or Redeemer, but at least each one of us having courage can say within himself, "Blessed be His holy name!"

This prevents the possibility of one falling into the same foul habit. And if one should himself fail in respecting the name he might quickly repeat not once, but five times, "Blessed be His holy name!"

For some there seems an excuse for cursing in that lack of education finds them struggling for suitable Anglo-Saxon words to properly express enthusiasm, anger, hatred, grief—or sometimes, even love.

Really, though, lack of education is no excuse. No one in his right mind is proud of any lack in his person. Why should this be an exception—that anyone thinks he has reason to curse?

Time was when men were ashamed to have cursed in the presence of a lady. Gradually, such shame has disappeared as the lady demanded equal rights for women! Now both sexes felt embarrassment for cursing only in the presence of a clergyman.

Isn't it strange that the "presence" of God is ignored by people who use His name without any reverence?

Today: There might have been a time when people were embarrassed for cursing in the presence of a clergyman. I doubt if that is any longer the case! But maybe, if the clergyman is like Christ, there is some embarrassment. I never could figure out why people don't cuss and swear when priests and nuns are around. Three cheers for anyone who submits the correct answer—if there is a correct answer. If I want to cuss, no priest or nun is going to hold me back. If I'm going to praise God's name, I'll do it because I want to and not because "Father" or "Sister" says it is the nice thing to do—but today I mean it, "Blessed be the name of Jesus."

Remember?

It is interesting that any reference made to the past is generally one of harshness. Even love songs, which ask us to remember, suggest a glorious past long forgotten. There is a certain despair in the lyric which advertises that unless one goes back to a happier day, all is lost—love can never be recaptured.

The same thing is true of moments that attempt to arouse national fervor. There is almost a monotonous prose in our history books which indicates that nearly every generation is goaded to action by a memory.

"Remember the Alamo" carried us through the Mexican War. "Remember the Maine" allowed Americans to hate the Spanish at the close of the nineteenth century. "Remember Pearl Harbor" was a theme which marked all Japanese as the most treacherous villains ever to deserve an atomic attack.

It is time for the memory to serve in a capacity which will arouse not distrust, despair and hatred, but rather faith, hope and charity.

It is time for us to develop not barbaric, but Christian memories: Remember Christ died for all of us. Remember He wants us to be one in Him and His Father. Remember He will give us the grace necessary for the day. Remember, "I will be with you all days, even to the end of the world."

Then with the good thief we can ask with assurance, "Remember me when you enter into your kingdom." Such uses of the memory allow us to penetrate a joyful future rather than a futile past.

Today: What a blessed thing it is to be able to *remember*. I remember my pre-school days at home with mom and dad. Then, too, I remember that first day at school, my First Communion day, my first car accident and the day I said FOREVER when I pronounced my perpetual vows. Memories of my parents, brothers and sisters help me over the rough days. Recalling touching moments with my friends gives me the courage at times to say "Lord, Thy Will be done." Today, I am going to thank God that it is easier to remember than it is to forget.

Alumni Month

It is a great tribute to any man when great numbers attend his funeral—and shed tears of genuine friendship. A man who has left no friends behind has left little else either.

On one occasion Christ said, "Let the dead bury the dead!" This seemingly impossible order is at first glance quite senseless.

During the month of November, we remember particularly the dead. It is logical, that as all nature dies for the winter, our thoughts should turn to death and the dead.

In November we are in reality saying, "I am alive. I am not burying the dead, but rather keeping all the good things they accomplished alive for this generation."

Each remaining friend keeps a part of the person gained in friendship. Just as we know of scientific helps we have which can be attributed to Edison, Fulton, or any number of people—so also do we have moral and psychological helps from unnamed and unknown people of generations past.

We do not think of Edison each time we flip a switch for a light or radio. Unfortunately, we don't think often either about the good people who have preceded us in the Christian life.

November, and particularly All Souls Day, gives us such an opportunity to remember our successful predecessors—and by our prayers show gratitude for a continuing inheritance.

Today: I wonder how many people will be at my funeral. How many will be there out of a sense of duty—because it will look good. How many will be there because they want to see who else showed up? Some may come to see if the mortician did a good job—used the right make-up to make her "look so alive." Just maybe—some will come because they really love me and want to see me for the last time. Maybe some will even come to pray for me. Who shall it be?

Veterans

This week Americans celebrate Veteran's Day. At least some Americans will. Others are not too happy that we have veterans.

It seems we are sometimes carried away by certain concepts of war and peace. Why Americans should prefer seeing a Second World War airplane, a Sherman Tank or a howitzer in a beautiful city park in preference to beautiful trees or shrubs is beyond my comprehension.

These are objects of war, death and destruction and add nothing to anyone's sense of beauty. On the other hand, plaques or statues honoring men who consider American freedom worth defending is another thing.

While we honor all veterans we do it not only with love and appreciation for what they have done in the past, but also with a hope that the future may one day be able to forget veterans as they might wars.

We honor the Gold Star Mother who would be pleased to pass up the honor and have her son still alive. We honor the war dead who would rather have lived without war. We honor those who have returned knowing they would rather have stayed home all along.

Whether we be hawks or doves, we all hope Veteran's Day will one day be merely part of ancient history, recalled to mind only by crumbling monuments unneeded by the human race. Meanwhile let us honor those who have answered the call to serve in a cause they considered just.

Today: In one way or another, each one of us is a veteran. Maybe we haven't fought in a war, but if we've lived life optimistically, hopefully and faithfully, we are veterans. Real honest-to-goodness veterans are those who can face life honestly day after day. I've never been to Pearl Harbor, Japan, Korea or Vietnam, yet I consider myself a 50-year veteran of life. Just what is a veteran? I'm not sure, but if Americans are celebrating Veteran's Day, I want to be in on it. I call anyone who lives life joyfully and courageously a veteran! Carry on!!

Yes and No

One question that is invariably asked of the priest is, "How can I say no to my boyfriend and still keep him?" In a time when popularity is at such a premium the answer becomes quite important.

The distinction must be kept in mind at all times that there is a vast difference between saying "no" to a situation and "no" to a person.

A girl, by kissing the hand of her boyfriend, may be interrupting a possible situation of compromise, but she is not interrupting her affection for him.

Christ does not allow us to say "no" to a person. He tells us to welcome the sinner—to love the sinner and hate the sin. Obviously, one shows the greatest love for the sinner by saying "no" to the sin.

Very rarely does one have to explain the situation. God has given each of us a conscience which quite accurately tells us what is right or wrong. Consequently, no one needs a picture drawn as to why one says "no" to sin.

The answer then should be clear. You never say "no" to the friend, only "yes." One only says "no" to a wrongful situation. If the person equates himself with such a situation, then you're not saying "no" to a real friend.

If one's popularity depends on a "yes" to every situation, his popularity is already non-existent. Real popularity is that which endures in spite of a definite resounding "No!"

Today: So I'm supposed to know how to say "no" to a situation without saying "no" to the person. It seems to me that a simpler solution would be to associate with persons who don't put me in situations requiring a "no."
Today I'll think about my best friends and see if my *yes* friends are also *yes* situation people. That could help me straining my *yes* and *no* decisions.

Thanksgiving

This Thursday, Americans won't necessarily be going "over the river and through the woods to Grandmother's house," but many will be taking a four-lane highway in that general direction.

Some of us thank the Pilgrims instead of Christ for this great time of over-eating—and strangely enough, this is as it should be. The Puritans or Pilgrims were not Christians. They did not accept the fact that Christ was God.

As a result of this, they initiated the original Thanksgiving as a reaction against Christmas. The early Americans of the Protestant and Catholic persuasions were so upset by the Pilgrims intent that their members were not allowed to celebrate Thanksgiving in colonial times.

It was not until the Puritans were quite extinct that American Christians adopted the occasion of Thanksgiving as a national holiday.

Changes in Christian concepts are not new. The early Church forbade candles and incense as pagan—in the catacombs they became a necessity. For some reason, now the necessity is gone, we keep the once forbidden as something almost sacred.

Thanksgiving, in a sense, is a yearly remembrance of the fact that there is good where one often least expects it. Too often we condemn others and their practices merely because they are not similar to our own. It is easy to forget that the people of Juda once asked, "What good can come out of Nazareth?"

This Thanksgiving, it may be well for us as Christians to recognize the greatness of this day which was born out of hatred for Christians. It has now become a day in which Christians can show special gratitude to God—the God of the Pilgrims and their own God. And let us pray that all future changes, regardless of their source, will be turned by Christians to the greater honor and glory of God.

Today: Thanksgiving or giving thanks, it all amounts to the same thing, except Thanksgiving comes once each year and giving thanks comes so naturally—every day. There are so many people to whom I owe thanks—so today I'll use some extra time for a few telephone calls, card-writing and a visit or two. We are all sure of today—being sure of Thanksgiving is another thing. My grateful heart overflows with gratitude today and everyday. Thanks to you and you and you.

He Cometh!

Anticipation is quite a human experience. It is awesome—wonderful or terrible. The most exciting moment of a date for the girl or the boy is very often the time involved before the date begins. Once they get together, things can become very dull compared to what each thought the reality would be.

The greatest moment in a football game is usually before the kick-off. The player waiting on the goal line for the boot has mixed emotions. He wants the ball to come to him so he can successfully return it for the touchdown—and at the same time he fears if it comes his way he may fumble the pigskin.

The most exciting part about Christmas gifts for the children is in the anticipation. The parents share the joy immensely. It is not unusual that little holes are punched in wrappings far in advance, packages are shaken and squeezed. Once opened, a certain joy is forever gone.

In Advent, the Church allows us once again to go back in history to the time before Christ. A time when the chosen people are eagerly awaiting the coming of the Messiah.

As Christians we think we know what the coming of Christ means. But we should ask ourselves whether or not our disposition even remotely approximates the attitude of Mary.

We can only appreciate Mary's Lent or Advent if we share her love for Christ. What foolishness we endure if we think we can comprehend the fantastic anticipation of Mary's joy if we don't have any of her devotion and understanding.

With Mary, our souls must magnify the Lord!

Today: He cometh!!! Young girls sit and wait saying, "He cometh." During pregnancy, mothers wait and often think, "He cometh." Mothers whose sons are out on a date wait for the least sound of "He cometh." Wives of alcoholic husbands lie frightened in the dead of night for the moment when "He cometh."
Mary's "He cometh" was different. It meant that for all of mankind, for all time, heaven would be ours.
Today I'll check things out to see if I'm counted in on Mary's "He cometh."

Seek and You Shall Find

If Christ were to come into the world today, in what form would he be acceptable? Would he be an American? An Asiatic? Would He be white or black?

In what neighborhood would He feel at home: Upper middle-class? ghetto? in luxury's lap? the street where you live?

Would he attempt to turn on the hippy generation? This time would He accommodate the establishment? Would the new John the Baptist be a politician? a teacher? a beggar? a philosopher?

Do you know any woman whom God might comfortably choose for His mother? Any man with whom she could be confidently entrusted?

How many conversations have you entered into recently in which you know Christ could be comfortable? Or have things changed so little that we really can't expect Him to be any more comfortable than He was the first time He came?

After two thousand years, the world is no more ready to receive Christ than it was before. If the world was prepared it would have Him. He offers Himself again and again to each of us.

Let us remember Christ said, "Whatever you do to the least of my brethren you do it to me." With this in mind, we must be cognizant of the fact that Christ comes to us again and again. Christ can easily be found today in the same place as the shepherds and magi found Him. Exactly where you least expect Him—if you honestly search!

Today: We've heard it so often, "Whatsoever you do—." Why is that such a hard lesson to learn? Just why can't I see Christ in my neighbor? I'll just bet that others don't see Christ in me either. That's not such a flattering thought. Maybe I'll get busy and do something about it. How about you?

Ask and You Shall Receive

"Is that ever a stupid question!" is quite often what we hear in conversation. Sometimes this is a response given in self-defense when one doesn't know the answer. Sometimes it really is a stupid question—but is it?

Each of us at one time or another has found himself fearful of asking for information because we are afraid someone will laugh. Much better to be the subject of ridicule and learn than go through life ignorant of truth.

It is well to realize that the one thing more stupid than a foolish question is not to know the answer. The price for knowledge is often an acceptance of the dunce hat.

An interesting study is to read the Gospels with an awareness toward questions. The woman at the well came to know Christ because He asked a question and she responded with many more.

Nicodemus came in the middle of the night to question Our Lord because of his position as leader in the Jewish Community. In spite of his trepidation, he received the knowledge of what was necessary for salvation.

Many times after Christ had related a parable, the Apostles would question Him further once the crowd had left. They received a greater fullness of truth.

John the Baptist, even though he knew who Christ was, sent his disciples to Christ with the question, "Who are you?" John used the question to introduce his followers to Christ that they might follow the Lord. Or as John so aptly put it, "Christ must increase, I must decrease."

Ask the question and walk from darkness to the light. Our capacity to know is limited only by our unwillingness to search. "Seek first the kingdom of God and all other things will be added."

Today: Fear is an agitation of the mind—in other words, "it is all in the head." It seems to be fear that keeps people from asking the right question at the right time. But if fear is all in the head, then we ought to be able to overcome it. Fear accomplishes little most of the time. It is kind of like worry. When it is all over, I wonder what I was all fussed up about. I pray that fear will never keep me from asking questions—even stupid questions.

Xmas

Until recently it always disgusted me to see Christmas spelled with an "X" instead of the saving name of Christ. Somehow the "X" indicates a lack of taste, if not more, for the Christian.

In reality the word Xmas may be more accurate in our times than the word Christmas.

Mathematics students for generations have been looking for "X." Nearly every problem is given with all the essential facts. Then comes the question, "What is 'X'? Find the value of 'X'."

For generations before the coming of the Son of God the Jews were searching for Him. They had been furnished certain facts by revelation. At His birth the shepherds and Magi were provided additional data which made finding Him easier.

Today, people are still looking for the unknown "X" in their lives. He is the answer for all the honest searchings of mankind. May the world learn to accept Him this Xmas so henceforth Christ can be the center of every person's life.

Today: My problem is, "What will I do if I find X?"

If I really knew the value of that unknown quantity, how would my life be different? Today I'll worry *less* about looking for Christ (X) and *more* about how to confront Him when we do meet.

I wonder what it will be like to really have found Christ? Will I feel like a shepherd? a king? an angel? or the Mother of God? What is on the other side of the equal sign?

Wanted: Enthusiasm

As the New Year begins it is well to face it as Christians—with the realization there is no such thing as Christian pessimism. Pessimism has no allowance for hope and hope is essential to the Christian Concept.

Unless we have an enthusiasm for life we cannot love God the giver of life. Unless we share an avid interest in all people we fail to see Christ as our common brother.

To consider anything more important than people is to reject the Scriptural Concept that man is the apex of God's creation—and it is to forget that Christ died that we might have more abundant life.

Gratitude for life, for existence, for being is often missing. Being ungrateful for life makes it impossible to give thanks for anything but death.

To live is more than survival for the Christian. To live is the opportunity to grow in knowledge and love. Because it is hard to imagine our non-existence we take life for granted and are thereby capable of mere survival.

In 1970 let no one be content with just being. Rather let our being be a daily expression of enthusiasm for the things which pertain to God and His people.

Let our Christian hope be so real and evident that the too often pervading pessimism may be dispelled. Let the optimism of the good news of salvation be in our minds and hearts in the year ahead that freedom may prevail with men.

Today: What is the opposite of enthusiasm? Whatever it is, I don't think I want any. I'd rather be enthusiastic—about my God, about others and even about myself. Today I'm going to try to be enthusiastic about my prayer life—maybe it will even work better. I'm not going to be a "reluctant" prayer but an "enthusiastic" prayer.

Dear Lord, keep me enthusiastic until I die—let me draw my last breath enthusiastically—because I'm coming home to you.

Allow a Samaritan

On every hand, one is constantly reminded that man does much suffering. The amount of pain in the world receives news but little relief. Perhaps one of the reasons we find it so difficult to give sympathy to a sufferer is the television advertising which leads us to believe that any amount of discomfort can be adequately compensated by any number of pills.

We are forced to ask the question, "How can anyone be so foolish to suffer when instant help and alleviation is as close as the corner drug store with some miracle drug?" We ask the question even though we, ourselves, might have a severe ache or pain.

The greatest tragedy involved with pain is our failure, at times, to communicate it. (Please, I'm not encouraging the chronic complainer.) Many of us do not have great gifts and talents to present mankind. However, each of us is capable of offering sympathy and compassion.

To refuse any communication about a headache to a friend is to deprive him of his ability to sympathize. It also makes one's actions and attitudes difficult to understand when the explanation is so simple and acceptable.

It is well to offer our daily problems and pains in union with the suffering of Christ crucified, but it is also well to allow others the position of Mary and John at the foot of the cross. Even Christ said, "I thirst!"

Today: What a joke—miracle drugs! I wonder who ever thought of that title, *miracle drugs*!!! But then—drugs would be miracle drugs if they caused *sinners* to become *saints*. Maybe some people need "miracle drug" prescriptions before they really get some spiritual sense knocked into them. If I would communicate to others "how bad I really am," they could help. With the help of others, sinners sometimes become saints. I won't get that kind of help at the corner drug store, but down the corridor—down the street where the retired people live. Old people are usually saintly people.

vintage '70

Holy Family

One of the greatest heartaches in the life of the priest is to be invited into a home to witness a family feud. The great tragedy is that the children are forced to act as the jury.

Parents who argue in front of the children force their offspring to decide against one of them. The fact is, the children generally vote against both.

If husband and wife are not loyal in their conversation with one another, little loyalty can be developed in the family.

Not long ago, a mother overheard her two daughters crying in the bedroom. She hurried to see what was wrong and was astounded when they explained they were upset because the two were having a hard time trying to decide which parent they would choose to live with after the divorce. The mother asked where the two got such a crazy idea. They answered quite simply, "Mom, everyone seems to get a divorce."

The mother assured them there was nothing about which to be concerned in their home. But, she wondered, how can one resolve the problem the girls posed.

It seems arguments in the home are sometimes necessary—and the results sometimes good. However, wouldn't it be great if the children in the home would more often see the making up after the fight— that even the greatest problems can be overcome with love!

Today: What a world this would be if even half the families would be HOLY families. But then—I wonder what makes a family *holy*? What makes a person a *holy* person? Is it prayer, kindness, love, or good will toward all? What makes a *holy* hour?

Maybe holiness comes from making up with people— from making up with Jesus, too.

Another Chance

Too often people complain when the world seems harsh and man refuses them another chance. Sometimes, out of a false sense of doing a friend a favor, another chance is given.

A loving parent who continually gives his child another opportunity may very well serve the child much better with a proper punishment. An employer could very well be doing an employee a great favor by firing him. If a man is not suited for his vocation or work he may be slowly but more certainly destroyed than if he is encouraged to remain in an unhappy situation.

Bing Crosby lost every job he ever held in his youth because he spent too much time singing—much to the distraction of his co-workers, and much more to the distress of his employers. No one, especially Bing, feels sorry that he wasn't kept on the payrolls. He made his fortune doing the very thing that cost him all previous employment.

Many great athletes, after being released because of inadequacy with one team, have proceeded to become super-stars with a new manager, coach and teammates.

And many a man who has been given a second chance with his sweetheart wishes it hadn't been granted—just as many are grateful the second time around was allowed.

Even God in his great mercy gives us no guarantee we will have another chance. In fact, to depend on it, is presumption! A man is foolhardy to go through life expecting another chance. Let us makes the most of each opportunity as it presents itself.

Today: If only I could get it through my head that some chance may be my last. Second, third, fourth, and *more* opportunities are so easy to get from *most people*—most of all from God. When my last chance comes, I want to be ready to say, "Hello, God!"

Tell Me

Sometimes it seems very embarrassing to receive any kind of correction. The fact is, it is easier to be corrected than to correct.

If one is aware of another's bad breath, he would rather suffer the discomfort of the odor than the discomfort of telling a friend about the situation.

It is difficult to talk with a lady who is dressed to perfection except for the fact her earrings don't match. One would prefer to hope this is a new style he is unaware of, than to tell her of the circumstances.

The mental anguish suffered by an employee when he is released may be minimal compared to what the employer must endure in explaining the man's shortcomings and failures.

A child must become a parent before he can appreciate the words he hears as he is being punished: "This hurts me more than it does you." For the time being the child is not too convinced.

In many cases a high school fellow or girl will continue dating, even though he or she suffers an unbelievably unhappy time, rather than tell the other person the fascination just isn't there anymore. It is easier to let things slide and then make certain one doesn't end up in the same college.

With these thoughts in mind it is well for each of us to recognize that anyone who corrects us either dislikes or likes us immensely—and unless we can prove otherwise, as Christians, let us presume all correction is, indeed, fraternal.

Today: Fraternal correction? The two words seem almost like a contradiction. How can I fraternally correct another person? When ought I to do so? If it is too difficult to talk about bad breath or unmatched earrings maybe I ought to start with things that are really worthwhile correcting—the unkind remark, the gossiping, the sarcasm or just good old laziness. Maybe fraternal correction is difficult because I don't love the person or the cause isn't worth it. I'll think it over.

Small World?

When Christ told His disciples to "Go teach the good news to the entire world," it must have caused them to relax, at least momentarily.

After all, none of them could possibly do that. It would be quite impossible with all our advanced scientific devices. How could they do it?

Whenever an order is general it can easily be shrugged off as impossible. To call everyone in the phone book is ridiculous: Lines are busy, people aren't home—and after all who has the time. But to call everyone in the block is difficult. You know it can be done. It is possible.

Is it possible that Christ would ask the impossible of His followers? Not likely. The truth is the "entire world" is different for each one of us.

For a little child, the whole world is the block in which he lives. For the sick person, the whole world might be a single room enlarged by the medium of television. For the teacher, the classroom may be his world.

You and I determine for ourselves what our entire world will be. It may mean a close knit group of friends, perhaps a city, perhaps a state or nation—but whatever our "entire world" is, we as His disciples have an obligation to bring to it—to think, speak, act and carry the good news to the four corners of "our" earth.

Today: Oh, oh, I just thought of the problem! Too often I make the *whole* world *just me*. It is easy to think and act as if I'm the "whole thing." On the other hand, maybe if I even thought the good news just to myself, it would solve our problems. If each of us made an effort to study and learn the good news "just by ourselves" then we'd be better off than if we just sat back waiting for someone else to come and *teach* us the good news. If I really *knew it*, I'd run around to spread it.

Male and Female

Man has established many divisions within the human race. They are, in spite of any attempts to prove otherwise, somewhat arbitrary: Black and White, Asiatic and European, Capitalist and Communist, Protestant and Catholic, Christian and Pagan, Eastern and Western, Republican and Democrat, Conservative and Liberal, and on and on.

Christ prayed that we may all be one and that divisiveness among men should cease. Because we refuse the Christian Message we have no peace, either of the individual or in the world.

We could make more distinctions. We could teach brunettes to hate blondes, children to hate parents, freckled people to hate the unfreckled, people on the even side of the street to hate those on the odd numbered side—and on and on.

When God created the human race he allowed one difference within it, that of male and female. This difference was not for the purpose of divisiveness but as a force of unity.

The only distinction made by God was done for the purpose of love. His design of difference was for unity and attraction.

Let us follow the admonition of Christ and erase the arbitrary differences created in the human mind by the strong but stupid force of prejudice. Let us rejoice in and return to the differences in humanity which God saw fit, that the unity for which Christ prayed might be achieved.

Today: Maybe we can go one step further—each of us can stop calling the *other* sex, the *opposite* sex. I've never been able to figure out just which sex is the "opposite" sex. We're just different and thank God these differences bring so much variety. Variety eliminates boredom so even if it kills me, I'll say—"Thank God for men"— Thank God for the other sex. I just decided I'm going to appreciate the uniqueness of *males* and *females* in this world. I heard there won't be any *sex* distinction in heaven.

The Whole World

Scripture tells us that in the new age "the hills will be brought low and the valleys filled—and the rough ways will be made smooth—and the crooked ways straight."

The Christian is generally persuaded that the new age began with the coming of Christ and consequently it must be here, right now! If this is the new age, nature has not responded as predicted in Holy Writ.

Science with its atomic power may very well level mountains, but in so doing it creates a tremendous number of deep valleys—valleys which separate man more than ever before.

It doesn't seem possible that God intended the valleys to be filled with litter but rather with kindness and hope.

The beauty of the mountain peak is more likely to draw men to a summit meeting than all the fear of modern weapons. The cool, clear stream in the valley will entice men to rejoice and share more certainly than chemicals arranged to destroy insects, weeds—and men.

It is important that we come to a fuller realization of the words spelled out so well in the song, "He's Got the Whole World in His Hands" before we, the human race, come face to face with the reality, "We've got the whole world on our hands!"

The New Age begins when we begin to respect all of God's Creation. To love the height of a mountain is to bring it low. To enjoy the depths of the valley is to appreciate it at every level. To make the crooked way straight is to anticipate meeting Christ at every turn. The rough way is made smooth when every man is treated reverently.

Today: I'm going to thank God for having the whole world in His hands. I hope and pray that He keeps it there. If humans get the whole world in their hands, they will have to worry about world fuel requirements, fossil fuels and maybe World War III.

Dear God, please keep all of us in your hands—both in this world and in the eschaton.

When I get to heaven, I'll even try to help you, God. I'll remind people to let you keep the "controls"—really, I will.

Give Them the Word

It has been said that old people read the Scriptures because they are preparing for final exams. Any student knows that cramming has value but it isn't quite so difficult if one has been keeping up on the daily work.

Every home has a Bible—and the odds are the Bible is covered with dust. If the dust is not present the indication is more often that there is a good housewife in charge rather than an interested reader.

To have the work of God at one's fingertips and not read the word seems the ultimate in the realm of the incredulous.

How many adults have to admit they have never even read the entire New Testament—let alone the Old Testament?

On the totally practical, worldly side—can you imagine paying as much as you paid for your Bible for any other book, piece of furniture, glassware, etc. and never read or use it? Not very likely. The Bible is a pretty expensive ornament when viewed only from the cover.

So it is a big book. That isn't an excuse for not reading it. Rather, it is a reason for getting started right away. In fact, if you are a slow reader, you may not have time to prepare for the final exams.

Today, after the Gospel, the celebrant is going to say something worth your Christian consideration: "May your sins be blotted out by the reading of the Scriptures." You have the word, now read it—so you can live it.

Today: The Bible is such a big book and the New Testament is so long, but it only takes an hour or two to read one of the Gospels. I've come to realize that my problem is that I look at too much at once. Today, tomorrow and the next day, I'll just look at St. Mark's Gospel. After all, Mark painted Jesus as such a human person—He got angry, He broke the laws and He ate with sinners. Come to think of it, Jesus and I do have something in common—"humanness." Jesus was human too—Mark says so.

Here Comes the Judge

Somehow he made it to church. He sat near the back behind one of the pillars—far enough away so his bloodshot eyes might not upset the priest and cause him to forget the lines of the sermon.

Actually it made little difference where he sat because he was soon sitting comfortably meditating on the sleeping apostles. Well, actually it did bother those within snoring distance.

Everyone knew he hadn't drawn a sober breath all week long. In fact, most thought he was almost as bad as they thought he was. But now it was Sunday and he, as usual, was at Sunday Mass.

He never missed Sunday Mass and this bothered his fellow Catholics. It seemed like generations had repeated the same words, "There he is! In church this morning and he was drunk all week."

Maybe my values are mixed up but it seems to me he is being criticized for the one good thing he accomplishes. Why be upset that the man attends church?

It takes an awful lot of faith to get to church with a hangover—and faith is still a virtue. It is time we start praising Man for his good points, not condemning him for his weaknesses.

Doesn't the Scripture say something like "Don't even let sin be mentioned among Christians"?

Today: What would Christians talk about if they didn't even mention one another's sins? Oh yes, there's beauty, joy, love, virtue, and faith. In fact, right now I can think of many good things about others—so, it is true, that I don't need to talk about my neighbor's faults because there isn't anything else to talk about. That's not such bad advice after all, "Don't even let sin be mentioned among Christians." That is, of course, the other person's sin. Why is it easier to talk about someone else's faults than about your own?

Aching Back?

Somewhere, sometime, each of us has been impressed with the story of Adam and Eve and the sin which caused them to be sent from the Garden of Eden as the punishment. Part of the punishment was to work, henceforth, by the sweat of their brow.

Because the connection of punishment and work is taught us, we look upon work as something bad. Yet, this doesn't follow. A child who is sent to bed for punishment learns, as an adult, to overcome his resentment for sleep.

Work is not a necessary evil, it is a joy. Accomplishment demands work and man without accomplishment is not fulfilled. Inspiration and perspiration are both important—but inspiration alone leads only to frustration.

A man who cannot work is mentally and physically incapacitated. For him we can have nothing but pity and compassion. He who cannot work, cannot ever appreciate its results.

Christ never knocked work. He even sought forgiveness for His disciples for harvesting on the Sabbath. Paul tells us the laborer is worthy of his pay—and doesn't he use a great deal of ink talking about good works?

Christian joy demands Christian work. As the first Adam made work a problem for mankind, the new Adam makes it one of the greatest sources of joy.

Today: Why do we connect WORK with aching backs? There's HEAD work, FOOT work, HAND work, none of which affect my BACK!!! Sometimes I think that connecting work with pain is "just in the head." Maybe connecting work with pleasure could also be "in the head." If it's not there, I'll put it there—I'll keep saying to myself, "Work is pleasure, work is pleasure, work is pleasure." Come to think of it, *work is pleasure.* Someday I may no longer be able to work—then what? Maybe then I will really look upon work as PLEASURE.

Friend

A speech professor once told his class that no one should ever begin a speech with the words, "My friends." Sometime, someone may stand up and say, "Name three," and it could be embarrassing.

Christ, in speaking to his disciples, said: "I do not call you servants but friends." Paul, at that time, was not yet a follower. Once he became an Apostle he was aware of his friendship with Christ, yet he often begins his Epistles with the words: "I, Paul, a servant of Christ . . ."

Friendship demands service. When one decides to terminate a friendship the question frequently stated is, "What has he ever done for me?"

Christ's life was a life of total service. He expects us to serve Him faithfully also. This is why He calls us friends. Paul understands the relationship perfectly and rejoices in his role as servant.

Anyone who is in love looks anxiously for opportunities to serve the one or ones loved. Love and servant have no problems in finding a working relationship. Love demands the concept of equality, but the equality is found in willingness to serve one another.

If a person is unwilling to serve he is incapable of proving love. Let each of us toward spouse, parent, child, friend, be ready to serve, that the reality of love might be always as present as the love of Christ.

The words of Satan in proclaiming his "freedom" from God were "Non serviam." I will not serve!

Today: I'm puzzled by the "good Father's" expression which says "friendship demands service." It seems to me that real friendship, real love makes no *demands*!! Love and friendship draw the best out of me because I *want* to give, I *want* to serve, I want to be the *servant*. I hate to think that it is *demanded* of me. My heart overflows with love for my friends. God forbid that they ever demand it of me. Today I'll think less about myself and more about my friends.

The Tree Revisited

"... and cutting branches from the trees, they strewed them on the road before Him." Thus does Matthew tell us about Christ's triumphal entry into Jerusalem.

The crowd praised Jesus because He had just raised Lazarus from the grave. Such a miracle demanded attention from people interested in life.

Today, we experience one of the rare moments in life when Christ is popular. He never preached or sought popularity for Himself—or His followers.

John tells us this was the occasion for the Pharisees to plot His death since the mobs were gathering on all sides to follow Him.

By Friday, the Pharisees control the mob. Now people will be able to say of the crucified, "Others He saved, Himself He cannot save." Lazarus lives—His Savior dies!

On this, the first day of the week, the people strip the tree of its branches in order to honor the Son of David. Soon, He will carry the trunk of the tree to Calvary, and as an act of restitution for the mob will Himself be stripped—and His limbs will replace those of the tree.

Christ, the Son of God, came into the world to make all things right. The first Adam, like the mob, took from the tree. Christ, the new Adam, restores the tree. Adam ate the food of death—Christ is the food of life.

Today: Good grief! I wouldn't know how to act if people strewed branches in my path. I have a sneaking suspicion that Jesus had trouble with those branches too! Then, too, I think of those poor trees—stripped of their branches. Tearing branches off the trees gave the Pharisees something to do while they were "plotting" to kill Jesus. The moral of their story was to keep their hands busy while their heads were "cooking up" the mess. It looked better. Today I will keep my hands quiet for one hour while my head does the work.

Happy Easter

Today, we celebrate the victory of life over death. Each of us may celebrate in his own way. (For heaven's sake, look at that hat, will you?) Regardless of how we do it—as Christians we celebrate life.

This is a day of mystery and searching. The mystery of the Resurrection—the searching of Mary Magdalen. (Mom, did the Easter Bunny come? Where is he now?)

When better to count our blessings as His followers and believers? Herein is the basis for our faith. (I have found twenty-three eggs. Do you think there are more or should we relax and eat these?)

Christ has proven love for us by His rising from the dead. He has given us all. (My wife's new outfit is really beautiful. She just wiped out my checking account.)

For centuries to come, indeed for all time, people will suffer martyrdom in His name. Nobly they will face lions, burning, beheading and untold deprivations. (Before I get that outfit paid for, she will tell me what the children's clothes cost. I'll forget my noon luncheon highball for at least six months.)

Some people will have opportunities to meet the Risen Christ. Some will accept Him, some will reject Him, some will not recognize Him. The travelers on the road to Emmaus recognized Him in the "Breaking of the Bread." (Father is giving an awfully long sermon today. It's hard to pay attention to his message when I'm not sure the ham isn't burning.)

Isn't it wonderful that we can bring the spiritual and the material together for the honor and glory of the Risen Christ.

Today: For one minute I will try to visualize myself face to face with Jesus Christ—looking directly into His eyes—thinking, saying nothing!!

What are my thoughts when I meet Christ head on? I wonder what His thoughts are! I'll ask Him! Jesus, what do you think when you look into my eyes? What thoughts do I bring to your mind? Do I cause you pain? Christ, somehow you left me speechless. Do I do that to you?

To Believe is for Man

Faith is a very strange and wonderful thing. Sometimes we have faith because we do not understand but want to, and we accept the credibility gap. Sometimes we know better than to believe in spite of ourselves.

To develop personality and character demands time and patience. It is much easier to believe in the power of a filter or a spray can for instant success. We call this faith, but it borders on superstition.

Faith is a reasonable assent to a truth because we trust a person as honest and reliable. Since men have a capacity to reason, it is logical for man to have faith.

In today's Gospel Thomas in lacking faith makes it easier for the rest of us. He insists on verification and receives it. Then he can say, "My Lord and My God."

We live in a world of faith. A child has faith in parents, a spouse has faith in the partner. If someone tells us a certain snake is poisonous we generally believe.

Americans are taught that a man is innocent until proven guilty. Consequently, it is easier for us to have trust and faith even though we are often fooled.

In our day there is a credibility gap to be filled. There are mountains to be moved. There are snakes to be caressed and poison to be drunk.

Daily, since Christ's death, He is betrayed and denied, yet mysteriously faith in Him persists. By faith, we come to the truth, we can move mountains, we can handle the serpent.

Christ allows us to believe that Christ has died, Christ is risen. And in us, through our faith, He can and must rise again!

Today: Snakes to be caressed!! That's going a little bit too far for me. I think I'd rather drink poison than caress snakes. But, I guess "believing" (having faith) is sometimes worse than caressing snakes. I'll never have my faith-life all together, so I'll use the faith I do have to say, "Lord, increase my faith." I kind of enjoy having some doubts and fears anyway. It keeps me guessing. It keeps me trying! How about you, my readers? Does your faith move mountains? Mine can only handle mole hills.

The First Day

Six days of the week we work hand in hand with our neighbor. We use the same shops, streets and schools. We enjoy the same restaurants and theaters. We cheer in the same stadiums and applaud in the same halls.

On the seventh day we do likewise except for an hour or so when we pride ourselves on our narrow-mindedness, shut ourselves away from the rest of the world and attend church.

It doesn't seem to work a hardship on others because they are doing the same thing in the search for salvation in a unique way while proclaiming all others ignorant, insincere or misled.

One day a week is set aside specifically to worship God and we often find in such worship a turning away from men—this in spite of the fact that Scripture clearly tells us if we profess the love of God yet hate our neighbors we are liars.

It seems unbelievable that Christ stresses unity so often and Christians have so little of it. He asks for one flock and one Shepherd, that they may be one as He is one with the Father.

The tragic fact is all too obvious. The greatest dividing force in the "Christian" world is the various "Christian" approaches to Christ. The non-Christian must be confused by the situation. There should be little wonder that he would not want to add to the confusion by joining the "Christian" confusion.

On the day of the Lord let us make a more honest attempt to be Christian that we can share the love and the joy as we do the rest of the week. Let us be as the early Christians who gathered together on the first day of the week.

Today: What an aspiration—to be like the early Christians!!
If I remember the Acts of the Apostles, it says that they did three things: (a) they prayed together, (b) they broke bread together, and (c) they shared all things in common.

The praying and the eating together isn't so bad, but the sharing stuff isn't so easy. I better get at it right now. Before I sleep tonight I'm going to draw up a plan of sharing ALL THINGS I have. Only then will I really be like the early Christians who were Christ's best followers.

Pollution Solution?

One good thing about air pollution is the settling of the race problem. In some places the air is so heavy everyone looks the same color. If we don't quit waiting for tomorrow to solve pollution problems perhaps every race—in fact the human race won't have many tomorrows.

It used to make me happy to see others smoke because it always was cutting the share of taxes I had to pay to support government efforts. But now when I realize how much shorter the smoker's life span will be, I know I'll have to pick up my share when they are gone.

One bad thing about water pollution is the temptation to think one is Christ merely because he can walk on the water. It is going to be hard to convince the next generation that water can come in three forms: liquid, solid and gas. Unless something is done soon it will all be in solid form.

God created the world and saw it was good. Such judgment is hard today because we really can't see the world. Christ came to re-create the world and we have generally done an excellent job of camouflaging His works and words also.

As Christians we cannot ignore our role of removing pollution from mind and matter. In a sense the whole problem needs one thing for its solution—Discipline. Unless we learn to control self we will be controlled.

Today: "To control or to be controlled," that seems to be the problem. Since I don't like to be controlled by anyone or anything, I better learn TO CONTROL MYSELF. I wonder how long that will take. I might not have too much time left so I'll have to accelerate my *self control* course.

That's the tough part about being sick—you never know how much longer you have. In one way, having cancer is better than getting killed in an airplane crash. It gives you more time to get ready for that "final landing" in eternity.

Freedom

Our American heritage demands the concept of freedom but our concepts are not always too clear. Somewhere along the line we have been persuaded that we are free to believe whatever we want—in spite of the fact that our experience dictates otherwise.

No matter how convinced I might be that the law of gravity has been repealed it still isn't the case. To step off the Empire State Building would be adequate proof the law is still in effect despite my desire to believe otherwise.

It isn't a case of being free to believe whatever we want. Rather, it is the fact that the truth makes us free. As a child, I may have been convinced that my little dime wasn't worth as much as my "friend's" much larger nickel. My ignorance was costly.

If a child knows a nickel is worth five cents—that a stick of gum costs a penny—that one plus four equals five—he is free to argue for four cents change when he purchases the gum. Otherwise he takes whatever is offered with no questions asked.

Christ says "the truth will make you free." He also says He is "the way, the light and the truth." To know Christ is to have the ultimate truth.

To accept or reject Christ is not an exercise in freedom but foolishness. To accept Christ and His teachings is to accept the truth—and freedom!

Today: I never could understand all that freedom stuff. Maybe that's why I'm glad there's a law of gravity, even if it takes away some of my freedom. God was really a "smart" God when He made gravity—and it's amazing to know that it always works. What goes up, always comes down. My God is really a powerful God—how about yours?

What kind of God (gods) do you have? Sometimes I confuse my God with my gods! Does that happen to you too? What do you do about it? I'm going to think about it right now, God or gods???

The Meek Shall Inherit

In Paul's Epistle to the Corinthians, he tells us he fights to enslave his body. He tells us also that he is running a race in an effort to win. There is something about both these concepts which leaves one uncomfortable.

Any track star will tell you that it is not a relaxing sport. Hour after hour he runs. At the training table he is diligent in following a strict diet. There must be the perfect balance so he weighs as little as possible without sacrificing strength.

He realizes, as does Paul, that each race has but one winner. But Paul's race is different since no one has to lose merely because another wins. The Christian Community is set in such a way that every winner of the prize sees that goodness is shared—that there is no victory if someone else fails.

To enslave one's body is only for the purpose of freeing the intellect and the will. Paul does not refer to enslavement of the person. Actually he is demanding personal freedom.

There is no freedom in sin. There is only freedom to sin—and Paul wants the only absolute freedom to love instead.

Too often we dwell on the rigors demanded of the Christian. Too often does Christianity receive a negative press. Christ taught us sacrifice, not surrender. We sacrifice out of love. We surrender out of fear. We sacrifice in strength. We surrender in weakness.

Christianity has never been for the weak. Christ asks us to be *meek*—we must not confuse the two concepts—or we are not Christians.

Today: That's right—Christianity has never been for the weak. It takes a lot of courage and a lot of strength *to get involved*. Life is so much easier when I "let George do it." It is so easy to look at someone in need and do nothing. Today I am going to ask God to impel me to action in moments of crisis. Unless I am willing to act, I'm a coward. Joshua (1:9) says, "Be strong and of good courage; be not frightened." To be Christian means to be strong.

Mother's Day

Not even the "self-made man" can explain away his mother. In fact, such a successful man is generally anxious to admit that in some way or another she had a hand in his success.

Have you children noticed how wonderful Mom is looking, acting and feeling today? Don't think for a moment that her motive is to get some special gifts from you and Dad. She would look, act and feel like that every day if you would treat her like every day is Mother's Day.

It must be the mystery in the entire history of the human race, that a woman will go through what a mother has to endure for three hundred and sixty-four days to be honored for one short day in May.

It is doubly strange when she generally does all the cooking and dish-washing that day, too. If I were a mother I would rebel. I'd cook the meals ahead of time, put them in the deep freeze, and serve them on paper plates. Or even worse, I'd insist on going out to eat so I could face a different maddening crowd.

You lucky people! Who else in the world would be so kind as your mother, in spite of your shortcomings and long-goings-on. You are especially lucky when you know how well she knows you and still loves you. You might say, "That is her role," and I agree. But do you know anyone who could play it more admirably—or more important, "Would you want anyone else playing her role?"

Today: How do mothers do it? They give children plenty of food and love. That's how they do it. I believe it takes a special generosity to really be a mother. It also takes divine help. Christ said, "Whoever receives one such child in My name receives Me." Comprehension of that thought ought to give mothers a sense of their high calling.

O Lord, it must be a job raising children! O Lord, be good to mothers.

Ecumenism

On the first Pentecost the Spirit was allowed to move where He would. No human beings had yet declared prior claims and sole access to the workings and messages of the Spirit.

Triumphalism is too often found within our various denominations. For any denomination to declare unequivocally that the Holy Spirit cannot possibly work through another denomination seems somewhat diabolical. To limit the Spirit is a denial of the omnipotence of God.

A closed mind is rarely opened by an outside force. All the arguments of theologians, regardless of their stature, will not open denominational doors unless the theologians are within each denomination.

Each group must furnish its own leaders who maintain an openness to the Spirit's movements within itself—and appreciate the Spirit acting through others.

Unless we are willing to allow freedom of the Spirit we have no right to expect the gifts of the Holy Spirit. For an honest ecumenism, there must be present the gift of Understanding in all interested members of the Church.

Christ never urged compromise. He came as truth. He insisted He "must go so the Holy Spirit could come and recall to all minds whatsoever He had taught." There is no reason to suspect that the Spirit of truth wants compromise either. Unity is not found in compromise. It is found in truth!

Today: It just struck me again that I have but one life to live. It just seems that I better live it without compromise. I better get off the merry-go-round and start on the straight and narrow path. Some day I'll stand before the judgment seat of God. That will be the moment of real truth. There will be no compromise then, so I won't practice it now either. Lord, help me today to be true—to live the truth!

The Word

When one goes to a ball game, he generally finds himself standing somewhat at attention for the National Anthem. Some sing with vigor because they love to sing. Others remain silent because singing is not their thing. Generally, the fact that they do or do not sing has little or nothing to do with patriotism.

The same thing is true about hymns in church. Whether one sings depends on the mood or the melody. As with the "Star Spangled Banner," no one pays much heed to the words.

Life itself is like singing. There are people who live because they feel they must exist. Others live because they want to live. As with the song, they pay little heed to the "Word" of Life in either case.

To be a Christian as though Christ, The Word, never existed is the ultimate foolishness for the "Christian." He said He was the Way, the Truth and the Light. To miss any one of these three things is to miss all real purpose.

Today, during Mass, whether you sing or remain silent, pay heed to the message. Listen also to the beautiful, meaningful words of the Liturgy. Years of experience have brought tremendous richness to the Mass.

Every prayer, every concept is packed with power. Yet, it is a power which can act effectively only if we accept the message freely. Life, like a song, demands attention to the word.

Today: I read once that on an average day most people speak about 48,000 words. No doubt many of those words are packed with meaning. If the words of humans have power, what about THE WORD that is God's? For most of us, there is no poverty of words, but only poverty of meaning.

Just for today, I'm going to watch my words. I'll be especially attentive to the words of the Liturgy and to the words of others. I may even begin to speak *less* so I can listen *more*.

Our Father

Morality is a family thing. One cannot think in terms of parents without considering the question, "Is what I'm doing pleasing to them or not?" Conscience generally decides an act is good or bad according to how one's parents would react.

The punishment meted one by a good parent is accorded out of love rather than anger and frustration. It isn't necessarily a question of whether the punishment and the mistake are in balance, but rather whether the punishment will help the child or hinder him.

Children, growing up, want to please parents, and hence try to be moral at all times. Parents, at the same time, are concerned for their offsprings' future and are living in an ever present attempt at giving good example.

When one is outside the family sphere he is not likely to be moral or immoral but rather amoral. He doesn't so easily consider his actions in relation to another quite so readily. During the time a person exists between childhood and parenthood he is likely to be just a hood—answerable to no one, in his own mind.

It is with this thought in mind that the father being reprimanded by his wife for punishing their child "too severely" could respond, "Better our son cry today, than his mother tomorrow!"

The same concept of family is stressed by Our Lord throughout the New Testament. He repeatedly stresses the fact that each of us is His brother or sister—that we are all children of the Father.

It is good to hear Him pray that we might be one in Him as He is in the Father—that we might be one in Them.

Today: Sometimes it is hard to know what this "being one in Him" is all about. It's much easier to say, "I'm me and you are you." But it was no one less than Jesus Himself who said that we must all be one in the Father. I'll spend a few minutes today thinking about how much I really care about others, especially my brothers and sisters. I really do care deeply about matters that affect the good of others, but I still must pray that I don't get so wrapped up in "me" that I ignore anyone else. I am my sister's keeper—Jesus said so and that's that.

Let Us Begin

There is a time in life when man has never sinned—when all the commandments are completely unbroken. It is the time when God is honored as our Creator and His Son as our Redeemer.

Children are obedient to parents, not because of any fear of punishment but because they have a deep love for the father and mother.

Such a love is deserved because the parents have a mutual respect for one another as vessels of election and salvation.

Men do not drink to excess and there is not heard even one quarrel throughout the land. There is peace in the entire world, not because all men are dead but because they have learned to appreciate life.

Purity of heart allows each person to see God in everyone—the God of love. Mercy is rare because justice in abundance makes it less needed. But mercy is ever available if the need arises.

Honesty is in each mouth. Sometimes, it is spoken with praise. Sometimes, it is contained and held, out of charity. Because man is not ashamed of his actions, he walks in the light and he is not afraid of the truth.

When is this time? It is not in the past. It is not in the present. It will only be so tomorrow. What we must do is to make tomorrow's promise present—let us begin.

Today: If tomorrow is going to be that sinless, peaceful day, I better have a good preview today. What must I do today to make tomorrow perfect? I could pray or do acts of kindness. I could work hard or sit and visit the sick. It doesn't matter much what I do—just so I do it in union with God, my Father, through His Son Jesus.

This is the day before tomorrow. I must use this day better than I used yesterday. How will you use your day?

Drink Deeply

"If your enemy is hungry, give him to eat. If he is thirsty, give him to drink." These words from the Scripture are seemingly demanding that we rise above pettiness.

Actually much more is being said here than meets the eye. If you have an enemy, you are automatically hungry. In fact, you suffer a dangerous hunger that is cancerous because hate has a way of feeding itself so well that love is starved and one is dead to Christ and His brother.

Hunger of the soul is total hunger. A man can be starving physically but unable to eat if spurned by a loved one.

Many a man is willing to go on a hunger strike in order to see justice done for himself and his fellow man.

A man without compassion and love—a man who is even his own enemy will often drink too much of the wrong thing and remain thirsty.

The Lord's promise is not dependent upon whether one is thirsty or satiated—but rather why. "Happy indeed are they who thirst for justice sake, for they shall be satisfied."

Such thirst sees that all men are fed and given to drink—not only of those things which will allow us to hunger and thirst again but rather that in tasting once of the love of Christ in our fellow man we will never allow ourselves the untenable luxury of having an enemy.

Today: Today I will spend five to ten minutes really studying my crucifix. A good, intense look at Jesus on the cross will probably compel me to do what I can, while there is still time, to help feed the hungry and give drink to the thirsty. Then, too, I will examine my own sense of justice. Jesus said if I thirst for justice, I will be satisfied. That is a good deal! Why do some humans need to be hungry and thirsty? I wonder what the world would be like if all people shared food equally.

"Dear" Old Dad

No matter where one goes in America today, someone, if not everyone, is receiving character assassination. The more important one is, the more certain the plot. It is part of an unhealthy national trend of despondency, frustration and pessimism.

It is hard to tell whether the image of the American dad is at a low level as a result of this—or whether the fact that the image of the American dad has been so often attacked that no authority can remain sacred.

The "funnies" in the newspapers portray dad as an underpaid victim, not only of his boss but of his spendthrift wife. He is the brunt rather than the source of the humor whether he be Dagwood Bumstead or the weak spouse of Pansy Yokum.

Television ads create a dad who is on a perpetual vacation from reality via the right cigarette, snowmobile, fishing equipment—or even worse he suddenly finds himself categorized as a possible future unfaithful if he just applied the right deodorant or drives a different car which will make him unresistible but not unresponsive.

It is a national conspiracy, dad. You can't possibly win. You might have a chance if you humbly ask help from the Women's League of Voters or some feminist group struggling for equality.

But until you are willing to take such a daring, humiliating approach, just don't pretend you can be a winner. And rejoice that today—one day of the year—you may not be a loser. Settle for a tie.

After all, wasn't it settling for a "tie" on the date of your marriage that got you where you are? You knew then you were picking a winner.

Happy Father's Day.

Today: Dear old dad—that's such a common expression but expresses a rather unusual attitude toward dads who are usually the butt of family jokes.

Why do people sometimes ridicule the father of the family? Is it because maybe we expect them to be too perfect—we expect them to give while not receiving signs of gratitude and affection—we expect them to be *where* they are needed *when* they are needed? Maybe dads ought not settle for a "tie" at Christmas, for

Father's Day and for birthdays. But then, dads wouldn't be dads, would they? God bless dear old dads today, tie or no tie!

Teenager's Psalm I

There is a great danger that each generation will write off the generation which follows it as being haughty and arrogant—unwilling to ask for help or accept it. This week and next the writings are those of a teenager:

What is Life?

Why is it such a small world, but it is such a big question? Really there is no answer to it. I exist in a world with no meaning. I wander around in a muddle. I hear no words. I see no people. I register no thoughts, but yet I exist.

Can life be beautiful? How would I know? Every taste is more bitter than the last. My heart beats because that's what it's been conditioned to do. It has no reason to go on, but it does. And so must I.

The wind blows my hair as thoughts blow my mind. It's a mess but it clears many things out and spreads them for others to find. Could everything just disappear and leave a ghost town in the cells of my mind? Memories come and stay locked in for all time to come.

Maybe someday I'll learn after long days of hardening my heart. Until then, I must go on. I will exist.

The pain is great. The hurt is worse. What of the scars they will leave? I realize the mistakes and it changes nothing. I'll always have visions of the good times, but they are shadowed by ugly words, angry looks, and terrible thoughts.

Why do I shake? Someone tell me I'm tough so I can stand the pain, the agony, the anguish. Why hasn't someone invented a band-aid big enough to cover this kind of hurt?

Nobody can help me. I have to heal the wounds by myself. Just let someone be there to tell me they understand. That will help. Pains go away, wounds heal, but what of the scars they will leave?

Today: So often we say to another, "I understand," but do we really? Can I ever really understand another's hurt and pain? Can anyone else understand my agony or my wounds, especially if they don't show blood?

It's easier to sympathize and understand someone's *bloody* pain than his *unbloody* hurts. I'll give it some thought today. I'll watch today and pray for all those who suffer hurts for which they have no wound or bloodshed to show. O Lord, make me sensitive to the hurts of others. Don't let me die with a hardened heart. Please, God?

Teenager's Psalm II

Sometimes, we sing because we want to sing. Sometimes, we don't sing because we don't want to. In either case we may miss the words. Sometimes, we live because we want to, sometimes, because we have to. In either case we may ignore the Word!

Of Existence, Of Life

Have you ever wanted to sit down and weep—not because something is horribly and tragically wrong, but because nothing is going right.

The sun doesn't rise anymore; it just struggles up from the horizon in a frustrating battle that leaves the observer exhausted. It isn't that there is no morning; rather, morning is just a drab grey extension of the night. It almost seems that the grass doesn't grow at all, it is too exhausted from the meaningless struggle for mere existence.

There are times when I question the hope and the meaning of life. Wouldn't it just be easier to close my eyes and let the same emptiness that is in my heart sweep over my body and mind? But I am caught in an ironic paradox of existence—"I have too many packages." "Put some of them down." "I can't. My hands are full." I feel so busy with little trivialities and meaningless activities, that I have no time to rest from them and live.

I must go on. But I am like a person lost in a blinding blizzard. I am so tired. Right now I would welcome a brief respite, an hour of oblivion, so that I would have the courage and the strength and the faith to live again! Help me God!!!!!

Today: It would be great if I could discipline myself enough to sit down and take one thing at a time. Why do human beings rush around so?

Sometimes I think that the greatest curse in my life is a watch. It's always time to do "this" or time to do "that." It's time for this meeting or that appointment.

Today I'm not going to let my watch run me. Maybe it will even be good for others. One whole day not knowing what time it is!!! That's the life for me.

Growing Pains

The old saying has it, "If the shoe fits, wear it." The implication is that such a situation is one of discomfort. Yet we all know the real problem starts when the shoe pinches.

Growth is a painful, exhilarating experience. It is hard for a child to leave the protection of parents and enter kindergarten—for awhile.

The mother loves the child no less if the birth was extremely painful—but she can "rejoice after her time has come since a child has entered into the world."

The educational process is full of hardships and rewards. The gradual recognition by the individual that he must constantly develop mentally as well as physically should be a cause for rejoicing, not tears, even though expending of energies is needed.

It is under duress that we best come to know the strengths or shortcomings, not only of ourselves, but of others. At such times the person's true personality and character come through most clearly.

We remember the answers in life which we have learned by mistakes rather than those which have come to us easily without need of our full attention. That is why we sometimes seem to find Christ more easily in repentance—because as Paul said, "He became sin for us," and allows us to come as close as the Good Thief.

And the Christ we gradually come to know best is not the babe in the manger, the child lost in the Temple, the great teacher or miracle worker—but the crucified Savior who in His great pains showed a complete love that we must grow to understand.

Today: People usually think of growing pains as something physical, but I think it is more spiritual. One's body just grows and grows and there's no stopping it. But the soul—now that's a different thing. One has to _will_ to grow closer to God. One must _desire_ to grow in grace. One needs to _pray_ to grow in love for God. Spiritual growth doesn't just happen. It's not like putting on pounds by eating chocolates or pizza. Spiritual growing pains can leave one depressed, discouraged or exhausted. It takes faith, hope and love to deaden that pain. O Lord, help!!

Share His Gift

It is interesting to watch a parent present his child to Santa Claus—then patiently listen while his offspring explains to good Saint Nick what his needs and desires are. The parent listens because he wants his child's every whim satisfied. To interpret it, we simply say the parent loves the child.

As Christians it is important that we become more aware of the fact that we are brothers and sisters of Christ—and children of God. As serious Christians we must show our love for one another by being as attentive as the indulgent parent to the needs of our fellow man.

Too often, as adults, when we consider another, we are more anxious to push another off Santa's lap and sit there ourselves, indicating our own desires.

Christ saw the greatest need for the human race was, and is, love. He saw to it that His love and grace is sufficient for each of us every day of our lives. If we lack the love of Christ, it is because we have rejected it. If our neighbor lacks His love, it is because we haven't shared it.

John tells us God is Love. God is infinite and therefore love is of the infinite. To be unwilling to share love is to refuse sharing the infinite—for by refusing such a sharing of the infinite we lose it ourselves.

If God is willing to share His infinity, who is man to refuse such generosity—and remain so finite.

Today: I'm going to try to realize what it means that "God's grace is sufficient" for me. If and when I really believe that, I won't fret or worry about a thing—I know intellectually that I am a child of God, but I don't really believe it with my heart. Sometimes there's such a big gap between my head and my heart.

I just got to wondering—does one love with his head or his heart? Does a person make decisions with one's head or one's heart?

Can I be generous with both my head and my heart? Does God give His grace to be used by my head or my heart? I wonder!! So much to think about!

Salt of the Earth

What woman has not used her entire supply of kleenex and both her husband's handkerchiefs at a "sad" movie and not exclaimed, "That was the greatest show I've ever seen in my life"?

What man has cried covertly or openly and not been ashamed afterward—as though man has no right to weep—that somehow it is beneath his dignity.

In pioneer times, someone had to pretend there was no danger, even though the wheels of the covered wagon were at the edge of a precipice, so the wife and family might feel a little unwarranted security.

It is foolishness to pretend that any era is not filled with perils—and sometimes it is more foolish not to cry about it. Emotion is a part of man's very nature and one should not be ashamed of his nature or his emotions.

If man is going to provide salt for the earth it is going to be by means of perspiration or tears, or both. The earth has need of man's salt.

When we cannot identify with our neighbor when he is in pain we are no longer capable of compassion. Compassion is an absolute requisite for the Christian.

Our model, the Christ, did not find it beneath his dignity to weep. He wept openly over the city of Jerusalem. He wept at the tomb of Lazarus. On the way to Calvary He asked the compassionate women to weep for themselves and their children.

Peter was able to weep for his sins. Judas was not!

Today: So that's the difference between Peter and Judas—their ability to weep.

> Ecclesiastes says there is a time for everything—even a time to weep. That ought to be a help. When did I last *weep* because of my sins? When did I *weep* because I hurt someone? What's happened to my sense of compassion? I just better give that some thought today. With a world filled with people who need compassion, I better not fail. Help!!

On His Blindness

A well known musical performer, who is blind, was being interviewed for a story. The reporter was excited about the added personal interest of the blindness. The musician made a brief request: "Please don't mention my blindness. I would rather be known for my ability than my disability."

Too many of us go through life complaining about our problems as though we are willing to settle for friendships built on weakness rather than strength. The consequence has to be weak friendship.

It is not so much that misery loves company but rather it identifies with it. It is much easier to identify with our neighbor's failures than his successes. For his successes we more likely have only envy.

Each of us can go through life identifying with disabilities. If that is all we look for it is all we will see. You can watch a man set a high jump record and dwell on your inability to be an athlete rather than rejoice in your fellow man's accomplishment. The greatest symphonic music in the world is wasted if one's only reaction is to complain about his own lack of timing.

If we refuse to see the good in the world about us and appreciate it to the best of our ability we truly would be better off were we blind. To see and not to see is the ultimate in blindness.

Today: Lord, help me to see what I ought to see. To see good in others is what the Lord intends for me. There are plenty of handicapped people in this world without my developing some sort of "good people blindness." When my eye balls get paralyzed, I better go pray for awhile. I'll pray that my vision returns—that my vision improves—so I'll never fail to see the good in others around me.

Today I'm not going to stumble past anyone. Others might even see some good in me.

Joy and the Lost Sheep

Not too long ago a priest answering the telephone heard the request, "Father, I haven't seen you since I helped build your church. Will you do me a favor and come down to this bar and talk with me?"

The priest's first reaction was to respond, "I'm here at the altar every Sunday. Why don't you drop in sometime?" However, he responded he would come right away. He entered the bar, collar and all.

Immediately, everyone gathered around the clergyman. All wanted to buy him a drink. He thought to himself: "I wish some of these generous souls were my parishioners—"

As he sat in a booth with his host the patrons took their turns sitting beside the priest. The theme was consistent—an urgency for reconciliation.

"Father, if you would help me I think I could solve my problem and get my old job back. I'm a master bricklayer."

"Father, would you come home with me and talk with my wife and me? She won't talk to me. I don't blame her. She's right. But I really love her so much."

"My kids don't respect me anymore. Would it help if I'd take the pledge? It kills me when they ignore me. I'd do anything for them. I'm just no good—but I want to be—for them."

"Father, I used to be an altar boy—'Et cum Spiritu tuo.' How about that?" The priest responded, "You haven't been around for quite awhile."

"Father, I want to get back to the Church. Don't give me a sermon, Father. Just help me back."

The next Sunday at Mass, the priest mused to himself: The people here don't seem to love me—or respect me like those who know the importance of reconciliation.

Today: I think there's a real art to reconciliation. When it comes to real reconciliation, most people *need people.* All of us can help others *better* than we can help ourselves. People need people to share their sorrow, their fears, and their hopes of being reconciled. I believe that life's heaviest burden for many people is the yoke of unforgiven hurts. This yoke can become lighter if someone else helps. Maybe this is what St. Paul meant when he said, "Bear one another's burdens." Helping others "to forgive" is part of sharing their burden.

"Going Unsteady

More time has been wasted by religion teachers trying to answer questions from high school students concerning aspects of "going steady" than by all other classtime-wasters put together.

Any discussion on the situation is foolishness since it is really quite impossible to even define what is meant by "going steady." From the point of view of the teacher there is the concept of exclusiveness and excluding—on the part of the teenager, the emphasis is on security.

In either case, there is an indication of selfishness. To "go steady" so one is assured of dancing every number while another dances not at all is anything but altruistic. To be resentful that one's "steady" would dance, or in any way communicate in a friendly way, with another is falling short of any Christian spirit.

"Going steady" is a situation that is absolutely juvenile. A mature adult never asks questions about the morality of the matter. A mature person is not insecure in his relationships with his fellow human beings.

When love is genuine and enduring, it is accompanied by faith. There is no envy or jealousy in mature love. There is an eagerness to show others the greatness of someone for whom you have sincere care. The immature would hide another's talents if it guaranteed exclusive "ownership."

People who boast they are going steady are unaware of their obligations to society. Those whose love is mature cannot think of love except in relationship to society. The adult, in love, thinks of marriage and family, the basic unit of society. The immature settle for a counterfeit called "going steady" as the established goal.

Today: I just made up my mind "to go steady" with God. Is that juvenile?? Not my kind of going steady because I'll have new obligations. On second thought, I don't think it is going to be so easy "to go steady" with God. But anyway it will be a worthwhile venture. I'll have to remember that most worthwhile ventures encounter obstacles, but I'm ready! I won't quit!

Paradise Regained

"I don't know you from Adam," may be interpreted in many ways, but it is generally not accepted as a compliment. It is especially a negative remark when addressed to someone whose name is Eve.

There are times in life when one doesn't want to be identified, such as when standing in a police line-up while witnesses to a crime are studying you with questioning eyes. On such occasions one doesn't mind hearing the words, "I know him not."

Theologically speaking it is indeed a great compliment to be considered so much like Adam that one cannot distinguish any difference. The first Adam recognized his sin and was ashamed. A man capable of shame is not all bad.

Every Christian has an obligation not only of being like the second Adam, but rather of as total an identification as possible. Our Lord is not uttering empty phrases when He prays that we may be one in Him even as He is one with the Father.

As stewards of God's graces and gifts it is incumbent on each of us to seek as total an identity with Christ as is possible. With this in mind, we are able to appreciate that the ultimate compliment a man can receive is to have it said of him by his neighbors, "I don't know you from Adam"—the second Adam, that is!

Today: I'm never too old to at least begin to be like Adam—the second Adam. I might seem a little retarded when I'm compared with Jesus, but at least I'm in the program.

Retarded people need special care and so, with God's special help, I might make it too.

Until I'm really like Jesus, I have something to live for. I really have a job on my hands today—to be like Jesus. I'll try to be so much like Him that people will recognize me as one of His followers.

Faith Without Works is Dead

We have too long spent too much time defending the fact of God's existence. In the Epistle of James we are told, "The devil believes and trembles." Our faith can be like the faith of Satan—to believe—except perhaps we don't tremble.

The fact of existence is not the important thing. It is much more important that there is some effect on us as a result of existence.

The reality of my parents cannot be questioned, but if they acted as parents only to the extent of giving me life and never furnished the essentials, such as food, shelter and clothing, then they are not really my parents since they have failed miserably.

The reality of God is not so important to us, in itself. The reality of God is important only if He is important to me.

If I live as though Christ never came into the world, as though He is not my personal savior, as though He is no different than any other person, His life and death has no value.

Religion does not hinge on the existence of God but rather that we have a relationship with Him which is vital. The role of the Christian is not to waste time in consideration of the Eternal Being but rather how his being can be involved in the Salvation history.

Religion is the acceptance of the most important role which man can lead. It is not the question of Christ's divinity but the sharing of it.

If Christ died and rose from the dead is not the question—but rather, how is my life affected by it?

Today: If religion is the story of God's love for man and man's response to that love then I better check on that response. It sounds like a good job for today. I'll take some time to think about God's love for me and my *vital* response to His life.

I want to improve that relationship while I still have the strength to do so. Father, help me never lose sight of why I'm really on this earth. My only important job is to love You and Your Son, Jesus.

Hypocrite vs. Hyppy-crite

Every generation looks upon the generation which preceded as hypocritical. When we read history it is hard to believe it is for real.

In the twentieth century one has to ask himself if the Christians really were serious during the Crusades when they shouted "God wills it" while they killed the Moslem.

The girl in the mini-skirt has to think great grandmother was worse than Victorian for her unwillingness to show anyone her ankle—even if it was sprained.

The generation now seated in the chair of criticism will soon be wearing the title hypocrite also, in its turn. And it will come as a shock because this generation like all which have preceded it looks upon itself as honest.

The "now" generation does bring one new image to the scene: "All honesty makes all things moral!" In the past when a man would set himself on sin he would keep his failures in the darkness. The "now" generation is different. If it wants to do its thing, have its bag, or whatever the proper terminology is—it is all right as long as it is done openly.

It is almost as though honesty, rather than charity, covers a multitude of sins. This hyppy-critical (to coin a word) approach is incredible. To think that a thing is immoral when done in secret and moral when accomplished in public is shallow thinking—and obvious self-deception.

How absurd can one be to think that all that is not done in secret is all right. Absurd is the kind word. The more honest word is brazen!

Today: I was just thinking that maybe I could stand a good lesson from "honest Abe." What a world this would be if all of us were 100% honest!! No one would doubt another's word. There would be no Watergate or need for CIA investigations. Politicians wouldn't have to wonder if they're trusted.

Help me today, O Lord, to be no different in private than I am in public.

Thanks to Abe Lincoln for his honesty in politics.

Moments

Isn't it wonderful that only God sees what we do? It would be so embarrassing if people cared enough about us to be concerned about our every word and action.

Isn't it great that your wife didn't see you put the empty glass in the refrigerator and the half bottle of pop in the dishwasher? Isn't it even greater that she'll never know who did it since the house is like Grand Central Station before the airplane?

Weren't you glad it was dark in the theater when you put your hand in the big ashtray at the entrance and played Ash Wednesday all over yourself as you made the sign of the cross?

Didn't you cover up nicely as you genuflected—as if you had just dropped the change and wanted to find it before it rolled way down to the screen—as if you needed it for the collection?

Weren't you chagrined when you sat solemnly in the pew and tried to find your seat belt? Didn't you rather wish you could have come up with a rosary or something?

Really, isn't it great that people couldn't care less whether or not you make a fool of yourself? Sometimes though, wouldn't it be much better if people cared enough to laugh when you are so ridiculous? Maybe, just maybe, people would be so much happier if they would just pay attention to people. We really are funny—and no one appreciates it. At least we can hope that God has a sense of humor—because He cares!

Today: Sirach says, "God lifts up the soul and gives light to the eyes." To do that, God first has to realize that I exist. People sometimes ignore others and act as if they don't exist. Now that I think of it—I do that sometimes.

Father in heaven, don't let me treat other people as if I were blind—as if I didn't even see them. Help me never to act as if I don't care and let other people "go it alone." Everyone deserves somebody else's attention! Always.

Stress

"Make up your mind." These words are spoken in the moment of crisis. Crisis is not a bad moment. The crisis of trying to decide what to order from the menu is wonderful compared to the situation when there is no choice.

Deciding one's vocation to the single or married state is a crisis much preferable to being forced by circumstances to remain single—or perhaps remain married.

It is not until the alcoholic faces the moment of crisis that he can be helped with his sickness. Up to that moment he must drink. He sees no other possibility. In fact, he refuses even to see a problem. Only a crisis allows him the opportunity of receiving the necessary help.

The major decisions in life are made in moments of stress. The student studies hardest under the threat of exams. The patient prays most fervently in danger of death.

The Christian message declares that we make up our mind. We face constantly the moment of decision. Our Lord says, "Those who are not with me are against me." That is why not to decide for Christ is actually to decide against Him.

He allows no neutrality. He demands that we "be hot or cold" or he will vomit us out of His mouth. Every moment in the Christian life is a moment of crisis. Every "now" demands a decision for Christ.

Today: Today doesn't look like a crisis day for me. But then, I rarely see "crisis ahead" when I arise in the morning. Maybe it is because I'm still half asleep—it could be that I can't see what's ahead or due to God's grace, each moment of life is a mystery, a real mystery.

Thanks, Lord, for the mystery of this day. That includes any crisis that lies ahead, too. It's so good to be alive that I don't even mind some moments of stress, some times of crisis. Each crisis increases my faith in the mystery of God.

Follow Me

There are times in every man's life when he can look at a fellow human in disdain. We can be upset by another's manners, his lack of cleanliness, sloppy grooming—and even perhaps his immorality.

Sometimes we hate to admit someone is even a part of the same human race as we are. Our reaction is so strong that we wish such would secede from humanity. Also, our reaction is so "natural" that we not only easily excuse ourselves but actually fail to see any element of pride in our thoughts.

From our point of view it even seems incredible that Christ could love some people, even to die for them as well as for us. Yet, the fact remains: Christ died for all men.

The Christ we read of in the Scripture actually found comfort in working with the undesirable—the lepers, the adulteress, those possessed, those with all types of physical handicaps.

In fact, the only person with whom He felt any discomfort was the proud man: the man who looked down on his neighbor—or away from him; the Pharisee who failed to offer the ordinary politeness; the proud person praying in the front of the temple, those who selfishly wanted to make Him a king.

This latter list is the one with which we identify when we look down on our neighbor. We are then the ones for whom Christ's death and resurrection has little value. Let us share the warmth of Christ's love by having compassion on those on whom he had compassion. Who are we to limit His love for others? His generosity?

Today: I will be compassionate today! Yes, I will! I said I would and I'll do it. For this one day I'll try not to limit God's love. Anybody can get upset—anybody can look upon another with disdain but it takes a pretty Christlike person to comfort Christ's special ones—the lepers, the adulteress, the retarded and handicapped and, above all, those professing publicly their immorality.

Today will be a good day—a compassionate day.

Now is Real

The undressed American is the person who forgot to put on his watch. All day long he looks at his naked wrist in utter disbelief. Not to know what time it is, is beyond comprehension. We are slaves of time.

We resent the slavery. We hurry through the present as though we are escaping an ugly past and have the assurance that the future contains only an improved situation for us.

With the first snowfall we are so happy that the summer is ended that we hasten to form the white crystals into our own image and likeness in the delightful figure of the snowman. We gladly compress the snow into a weapon, that we might knock the last leaves from the tree that it can be buried in greater beauty—the snow blanket.

The same delightful substance soon becomes the source of our melancholy and we watch the children with happiness as they push ice and snow in the water currents to hasten noble and conquering Spring.

We envy our neighbors who spend the cold winter months in the heat of the South—and during the hot summer they can afford to visit the frigid areas of some distant Northland—while we stay at home and freeze or swelter in due season.

Christ is not concerned with the when and the where as He is with the why and the how. The amount of time we have is unimportant when compared with how it is used. Let us not hasten the season with hope so much as live in the season with faith and love.

Today: It's not the quantity of time I have in which to love God. It's *quality time* I must have. Time spent visiting with some people is *quality time*. Time spent reading some books is *quality time*. Sometimes even sleeping is *quality time*.

Today is *quality time* if I use it *in* faith and *with* love. It really doesn't make any difference how many times I tell God that I love Him is my expression of love is of such quality that He gets my message the first time. Lord, I do love you with a love of good QUALITY.

Freedom

The cheaper life is held in esteem the more we are afraid to die. It is only in moments when life is held dearly that man can say, "Give me liberty or give me death." It is the slave who is afraid to die. He may be a slave to drink, to drugs, to flesh, to money—to what have you.

The free man, the lover and possessor of liberty, is not afraid. It is precisely the moment that man finds nothing worth dying for that there is also nothing for which he has to live.

To risk living is to risk death. One cannot separate life and death. Each is necessary for the other. To die is the final act of living.

If, from the natural sense of patriotism, we might prefer death to subservience, how much more must we value death as Christians. The great moment of Christ's death was prelude to His rising from the dead.

Ignatius of Antioch, at his death, said, "The blood of martyrs is the seed of faith." Because he had lived a long life in Christ, he was happy to die in Christ.

Many years later, Francis of Assisi, in handing us a prayer beloved by all, concludes his thoughts on peace with the phrase, "For it is in dying that we are born to eternal life."

For the Christian, death is not so much the conclusion to this life as it is the beginning of the next. The words of Christ impel us to fear not death—except the death which involves the soul.

Today: Sometimes I try to convince myself and others that I don't fear death. At other times I know that I really do fear it—just a tiny bit. I'm glad of that—thanks, God, for giving me just enough fear of the unknown that I don't get cocky about dying. It can seem so close and yet so far. Sometimes I want to die "right now" and sometimes I don't ever want to die.

Total renunciation and abandonment at times lead me to say, "Lord, I don't care when I die, just so You are with me when I do." After all, I'm just going from one life to another life—eternal life.

Existence Plus

Each year, on that particular day of our birth, we celebrate the fact that we are growing old. As children we don't advert to this fact since friends and relatives distract us with gifts in honor of the occasion.

Children logically await the day of restitution on which parents pay an extra price for having subjected their offspring to life.

Teenagers logically await the day of their majority so they can eat, drink, be merry, and vote with the other taxpayers.

To a certain point, age is important. It dictates when we can aim a car, get drafted—into the service or marriage—and according to one's constitution he can anticipate these birthdays with gusto or disgust.

Adults logically remember and await the day but more logically forget its number as they celebrate not an anniversary of birth but a commemoration. Once one is an adult, he ceases celebrating his age and more wisely celebrates his existence.

One's birthday in Christ, Baptism, is the time to celebrate his existence in Him. Families who have the custom of remembering the birth in Christ rather than, or in addition to, the physical birth are saying much more about existence. For them, the number of years in His grace can always be faced with joy.

It takes on the aspect of wedding anniversary rather than birthday because the anniversary is to renew a relationship with a person. Let us remember our spiritual birth in Christ with joy rather than our physical age with trepidation.

Today: If I really understood what it means to be baptized—to be a child of God—there would be no obstacles which I could not overcome. Religion books tell me that Baptism is a special Sacrament celebrating my birth into the Church community.

To understand what the Catholic community is all about many of us need visible signs. These are sometimes called Sacraments. Through these signs Jesus gave His Apostles special power so they could serve the people by continuing the action of Jesus among men. Oh, yes, that's it—my life's job is to help continue the work of Jesus. I still have "existence plus" until I die. Thanks, Lord.

Exit Reality—Not Laughing

There is only one reason for using drugs and that is to escape. Under a doctor's care, drugs allow one to escape pain, to escape sleeplessness and tension, to escape overweight—and sometimes, temporarily, eternity.

Without prescription, to a certain extent, the same goals are attempted. People use drugs to escape the pain of non-acceptance and the pain of failure. If one fails to be wanted and successful without drugs, then he can be put to sleep from reality with drugs. He is less acceptable but also less aware of it.

When someone lacks a desired ability, he can turn to drugs. The ability is not received, but the desirability is removed. Hence, no frustration even though ability is lessened or altogether lost.

An inhibited person wanting to change finds no change in the fact but rather the acceptance of the fact. No one is more inhibited than a heavy drug user. Drugs bring all users to a common denominator: loss of drive!

Christianity demands that we acknowledge our failures and shortcomings and accept things as they are.

Our Lord pointed out the beauty of work—even work resulting in failure. He did the same for all of life in general. God gave us our drives and expects us to use them intelligently for the good of all men.

Life has become too simple when only one drive remains: the drive to maintain the high cost of escapist living on drugs.

Today: So there's a message here about drugs. That's my bag these days—drugs and chemo-therapy. Drugs may do all the things the good "Father" says they do, but some of them also cause nausea, vomiting, sleepless nights. They also help a person face the reality that there is something wrong—like maybe the person has cancer.

> Victims of cancer are called to grow, just like stroke victims are called to grow. They are called to grow in their values, beliefs, character and temperament which makes each of us who we are. The greatest challenge of

my life is to live with lymphoma and yet be interested in helping to change things that need changing in this world. I can still say "Yes, Lord."

Thoughts

After spending millions of dollars on hair dye and diet pills, wrinkle removers and hidden hearing helps, contact lenses and foundation garments for the purpose of maintaining "perpetual" youth, it isn't at all surprising that one would want to think as a youth, also.

In spite of advertising, the young look like the young, and the old who try to maintain cosmetic youth would be better off sagging in antique comfort.

If we delude only ourselves in looking young, we make even greater fools of ourselves by the dishonest attempt of "thinking" young. It does not make me a member of the Pepsi-generation, even though we are about the same age.

Sadder and no wiser parents are those who abandon their own experience and their children in an effort to think as their offspring think. It is not impossible or even unlikely that the young have much to say to parents—but not enough that any sane parent should abdicate his reason and experience and not talk as a parent to the succeeding generation.

A family demands an exchange of ideas, not a mouthing of thoughts by just one part or party. Where there is no exchange, there is no family. If parents continue abdicating the role of teacher and assume the sole role of pupils, then experience is no longer a teacher at all, let alone the best teacher.

There should be little wonder that parents today so often fail in receiving parental respect and honor, since they so often have abandoned parental responsibility. It isn't so much a matter of thinking young or old. It is, actually, a matter of just thinking. Thoughts spring from a mind which is young—not immature!

Today: What a joy to sag in antique comfort—with or without a "foundation garment." Dear old people—sick people who are in antique comfort can still TEACH. In fact, that kind of teaching seems better. People listen better to a sick teacher sometimes!! They even can learn the Good News from the eyes, the lips and the heart of a dying person. No one should ever stop teaching, because teaching requires thinking and who wants to stop thinking? Jesus needs the sick and infirm, the alcoholic and the mentally retarded to help witness to Him before all nations.

Today I can courageously say, "Thank you, God, for my life—all of it—health, sickness, joy, pain." I really mean it.

Give the Best

Parents who are deserving of the title of mother and father want their children to have the very best that society can provide. Also, they want each successive society to be better than the one in which they were reared.

This kind of thinking allows us to too easily discard the things of the past, whether they be good or bad. Those who "think progressively" think all change is good, no matter what is lost. Those who "think conservatively" consider change the greatest evil. We need a generation which is willing to change when the change is an improvement—to resist change when it has no positive value.

In parents' efforts to give their offspring the best, they generally try to give them the things which were unavailable to themselves as children. In this they err seriously.

It is indeed foolish when adults try to give their children what they did not have, rather than offer them the things they had. An old Latin adage, "Nemo dat quod non habet" (One cannot give what he does not have) is too reasonable to ignore.

Parents who have children of high school age and over, knew want and hardship. They survived because they were taught that "Man does not live by bread alone." The lesson was well learned but generally not handed on. In urging the successive generation to grasp the material things of life, the spiritual is often neglected.

The intangible thing called "faith" has not been transmitted—and when one lacks faith in God, how can he have it in his parents, friends, teachers, country . . . ?

The tragedy is the attempt to hand down what one does not have and to neglect handing on what one has—especially when that something is faith.

Today: What did Jesus mean when he said, "Man does not live by bread alone"? He must have clearly meant that man needs something more than bread. Maybe Jesus meant that man needs more than material things. I get it: Man needs spiritual food too. What attitude do I have towards spiritual food? To answer that, I might have to examine my attitude toward the Church and its Tradition.

What do I believe?? Oh, oh, the search is on once again. When did I really search into my life the last time? What is my search history report? What people search for tells us what they are looking for. Sometimes it's God, or grace, or peace of mind.

Today will be a search day for me. I'll search till I find God.

Oblivion?

Man is ever striving to reach the ultimate of his potential. In considering the fact that one is made to the image and likeness of God, it is rather frightening what that potential is.

Philosophy and theology tell us that God is the Creator. Man in the pattern of God works at creation. In begetting the next generation, man has shared in creativity.

In modern society, such creativity is frowned upon. Anyone who wishes to procreate is practically ostracized for his family.

Man must create—if not children, then ideas. Each of us has an innate desire to leave a monument. A building, a business, a road, a bridge—something that will tell the world we were here. For a few it is sufficient to carve initials on a wall or a tree. Others are content that a proper tombstone indicate a past existence. Most of us demand more. Children is the obvious answer. If not children, what then?

A generation not having children must produce something worthwhile and lasting. This is why man must study and work. This also is why man must learn more and more to compliment others for endeavors.

Also, if man is going to refuse to propagate, he must be prepared to accept failure more easily in his life. The celibate has never had offspring he can point to as his heritage or monument. He has always been more subject to frustration. He has learned to accept this, or he is a misfit.

Our present society is forcing even many married people into the same circumstances. Is it any wonder we have so many suffering from an identity crisis when all one can identify with is failure to leave a monument?

Today: When I'm dead and gone, I wonder how people will really know that I was here. On second thought, I realize that every day that I am alive I continue to add to my obituary. What am I writing? What will my records say? What will people think I gave my life for? For self? For others? For the Church? Will they say, "She was a dreamer and couldn't see things as they really are"? Will they say, "She was a dreamer and was willing sometimes to pay the price to make them come true"?

Today I'm going to spend some time thinking about God's dream for this world. And God stepped out in space. He looked around and said: "I'm lonely—I'll make me a world." God's creation started it all—God's providence will end it all. So much to be happy about.

Christ the King

The ruler of any kingdom has laws established which are followed by his loyal subjects. In the kingdom of Christ, He makes much of the point that His followers are not to be considered as servants but as friends. His kingdom is based solely on the principle of love.

Love is an acceptance of a two edged sword. People in love know a price must be paid. The greater the love, the greater the cost.

Christ proved His love by the ultimate giving of His life in a most painful way. It isn't expected that we search to return that price—but there is the other edge of the sword—our means of proving love for Him—the keeping of the commandments.

Moses accepted the decalog, in the name of the Jewish people, as a treaty between God and the chosen people. He was to be their king as long as they would be loyal to Him. He was to reward them with His protection.

In the Book of Exodus, when the people are loyal to the commandments, God in speaking to Moses refers to them as "My people." When they depart from the law He says, "Moses, your people." It is almost like a parent who accepts an offspring's good qualities as being derived from him while the bad characteristics are of the spouse.

The ten commandments still stand. The emphasis has changed. They are no longer viewed as negative but rather as a positive force. "Thou shalt not" gives way to "Thou shalt."

Christ the King gives us two commandments: Love God and love your neighbor. In the new kingdom the motive is not fear. It is love!

Today: I'm going to compare the ten commandments with the eight beatitudes of St. Matthew's Gospel. One tells me what I can't (shalt not) do and the other tells for what I will be blessed. "Blessed are those who hunger and thirst for justice" and "Blessed are the peacemakers."

Am I a *giver* or a *taker* in this world? Do I continually give of myself to the world or do I take from others just for myself? I am free to give or take. It's my responsibility. Help me, Lord, to be a giver today—a giver of a smile, a touch of the hand, a giver of a telephone call or maybe a moment of silent prayer for all God's people. I can give until I take my last breath. Today I give!!

Thanksgiving

Somehow, we celebrate the holiday of Thanksgiving year after year with a strangely foreign concept of the feast. Foreign, that is to say, to the original spirit of the Pilgrims.

We recollect incidents from the lives of these hardy settlers—of Governor Bradford who ruled so wisely, of John Alden and Priscilla— and the "Speak for yourself" line.

We visualize the native Indians gathered at the original meal honoring the newly established friendships. Above all, we see the settlers as being happy just for their continued existence in the New World.

We remember with them the trials and tribulations endured in England and Holland, their trepidation and faith over the unknown ahead of them in coming to America.

In calling to mind all these things we do well. However, it is likely we are not actually celebrating the Feast of Thanksgiving in its pristine spirit.

It is possible we are being thankful to the Pilgrims for getting this occasion started on an annual basis. It may be we are being grateful to a government that calls business to a standstill so we can relax.

Or perhaps we, in the spirit of the originators of Thanksgiving, may be just plain grateful to a kind and merciful God—Who, in spite of great hardships, allows us so much as Americans.

Today: Thanksgiving as a holiday comes once each year.
Thanks-giving for all of life and God's gifts never goes away. I continually give thanks to God, to my parents, brothers and sisters, to my fellow religious and friends for their relationships with me.

I just realized that I am the sum total of all my relationships. That makes every person who has ever known me partially responsible for who I am. To all these people, I continually give thanks. I do not reserve my thanks for one day in the year.

Today I will be just plain grateful for all I have and won't worry about what I might not have. I love life—maybe I'll love death even more.

Identity Crisis

John the Baptist, in today's Gospel, sends his disciples to ask of Christ, "Who are you?" Christ does not give a direct answer. He merely relates what is happening in the world as a result of His presence.

John's followers seem satisfied with the answers given and they return with the news to the Baptist. There is, however, an aside which can easily be missed.

Christ does not clearly state Who He is, but He does clearly state who John is. The lesson is simple: we cannot really know ourselves until we have learned of Christ!

If I have never competed in a race, I have no idea whether I am slow or fast. Even if someone "clocks" me, it means nothing unless others have also been timed.

We all recognize that "in the valley of the blind, the one-eyed man is king." All seems relative because we have relative values. We can always look good compared to someone, even though it often requires making that someone up.

Once we know Christ we see ourselves in a new and more complete light. His simplicity leaves us confused, His growing in wisdom and knowledge and grace makes us stagnant, His suffering shows us selfish or perhaps unselfish, His love shows us unworthy or happy recipients.

So often today a man fails to know himself because he has failed in allowing an encounter with Christ. For our own sanity's sake, let us learn of Him.

Today: What does an encounter with Christ mean? Does it mean Christ is against me? Does it mean Christ is stronger than I am? Does it mean He is more solid and stable? Whatever it means, it involves giving up something and receiving something. Every encounter in life involves a giving of oneself and a receiving what another has to offer. Christ has something to offer me. I have something to offer Christ. What a sobering thought. It's so sobering that even alcoholics and drug users might like to use it.

Today I'll try an encounter with Christ—one at a time, taken when needed, or as directed. Encounters are medicinal.

Judgment Gap

Some time ago my nephew asked the question, "How do grown-ups expect us to understand them when they don't try to understand us?" Now the question and the questioner are different. Middle-aged people are asking, "Why doesn't youth ever listen to us?"

One answer often given is that no one over thirty has anything worthwhile to say. They don't try to understand us; why should we pay attention to them?

Obviously, the shoe must have changed to the other foot. Old people are trying to understand the young—the young, in general, couldn't care less what is in the mind of the elders.

The great problem is hasty judgment—or even worse, prejudgment. For the first time on the American scene, a man can be guilty because of age—be he young or old.

The question which must be faced by any person is this—"Am I so intelligent that I already know everything my neighbor has to offer?"

Is it possible that any man or group of men are so learned that he or they need listen to no one for the sake of knowledge? Not likely.

Perhaps the real problem today is that too many of us think we already know what everyone else has to offer—and if we never listen to others, we can continue fooling ourselves.

Humility says, "Know thyself." We cannot have even the beginning of humility if we are unwilling to listen to others' appraisals.

The American scene needs a return to humility. Knowing oneself demands a listening to others. The fact that God gave us two ears and one mouth should tell us that to listen is twice as virtuous as to talk.

Today: "Knowing oneself demands a listening to others." That's a simple declarative statement. It has a subject and a predicate. Both are important—knowing oneself and listening. But probably the most important phrase is "to others." I wonder why it is so hard to keep my mouth shut long enough to really listen to others. God's well-planned ratio of 2-1, ears over mouth, still doesn't do the trick—even for those over 30!!

Today I am really going to look others straight in the eye and listen. Anyone who comes in my path today better have something to say. My mouth will be shut more and my ears open.

Edifice and Edify

There is one day of the year more than any other which is family day and that is Christmas. If one cannot be present with the family, he at least makes an effort to telephone. Those at home await the call.

The first Christmas was begun by Mary and Joseph, miles from Nazareth where they had received God's message and were married. The census ordered by Caesar moved them away from the house of the carpenter.

A great lesson comes forth from the warmth of the stable. Home demands more than the protection of roof and walls. It demands a unity of spirit rather than mortar or nails. Home is more than a gathering place for meals. Our prisons provide as much. Home is established not by the heat of the hearth but by the warmth of the heart.

Wherever one's heart and mind turn at Christmas is home. Truly, home is where the heart is. That is why each Christian, at Christmas, finds comfort next to the Babe of Bethlehem. For here is the heart which will eventually be pierced by the failures of the human race. Here is the Mother of tenderness and her faithful spouse.

In the beauty of a moment called Christmas we have clearly been shown the distinction between a house and a home.

Today: A house may be an adobe hut or it may be a ranch style duplex, but it is still just a house. It's not the style of the house that makes the home. A home is where I'm wanted, where I'm loved and teased. A home is a place for noise and laughter, gentleness and intimacy. Come to think of it, a home doesn't even need a house. People who think houses are so important are dead wrong. It's not the house in which I live that makes me saint or sinner. It's the home in which I live. Today I'll spend some time in solitary confinement re-examining my contribution to home life.

Houses must decrease; homes must increase.

Sing and Pray

One of the greatest differences in the Church since the Second Vatican Council is in hymns. The difference is not only found in the change of emphasis from a choir to the people but also in the words.

There is little question but what it is easier to train an unwilling parish to sing together than it was to persuade individuals to join the choir. This gives some an idea of how hard it was to get new choir members.

Before the Council, the words of the hymns made God inaccessible. There seemed a difference between the height of God and the depth of man that no soprano could reach up to or bass fathom.

While this was frightening and disconcerting, the present situation can leave one even more uncomfortable. For now God has been taken from the clouds, and the hymn forces us to see Him in every neighbor.

Unfortunately, the end result (of the attempt to close the gap between God and man) has more often been a dehumanizing of Christ rather than a divinizing of man.

Unless we heed the Scriptures, we can be easily misled. We are never asked to search for man in God; but, on the contrary, we are told to see Christ in all men.

It is not, "Whatsoever we do to Christ we do to our brother," but "Whatsoever we do to the least of our brothers we do it to Christ." With this in mind the reality comes: We cannot avoid God!

Today: That Vatican Council turned more things around than just the altar and the priest. It has caused monotones to pick up and use hymnals. It even has people who can't look into each other's eyes shaking hands with each other and saying "Peace."
Why do Christians find it so hard to look directly into someone's eyes—hold their hand and say, "May the peace of Jesus Christ be yours."
Today I will make a special effort to capture the spirit of the Vatican Council in any way that it affects me.

vintage '71

Communism Revisited

It is a mystery to me that Communism has gained such a privileged position in the mind of modern man. If there is any answer why the followers of Karl Marx are allowed to glibly mouth their phrases for the benefit of "sophisticated" ears it may well be that time and propaganda have allowed us to forget that Communism is a religion—or more accurately an anti-religion.

The great attack on the American system may or may not be warranted according to the situation at hand and the circumstances involved. But to translate these attacks as a plus for Communism or socialism shows an incredible lack of insight.

Christianity has been able to survive any and all types of political situations. In fact, it thrives under persecution better than with benign considerations. Our religious orders are socialistic in nature so the politics of Communism should not bother us.

For Christians, it is not the choice between Capitalism and Communism that is all important. Rather, it is simply the choice between Atheistic Communism and Christianity.

Communism, as conceived in the mind of Marx, was anti-religious. Regardless of its geography or time-piece, things haven't changed. In his encyclical *Atheistic Communism* Pope Pius in 1931 made it clear: "It is intrinsically evil."

Today: People seem to either be all FOR or all AGAINST Communism. That's good because Christ tells us not to be lukewarm.

> It takes more than lukewarm water to make instant anything—coffee, oatmeal or soup. It takes water that is boiling hot. I've never given much thought to how useless lukewarm water really is. It's just that way with Christians, too. When they're lukewarm they're useless—apt to be vomited by Jesus Christ. What a sobering thought—it's better to be cold than lukewarm—better to be anti—than half-baked. Wow!!

Belonging

There seems to be an obvious contradiction in man that causes him to exclude others whenever he establishes a community. The word community denotes a coming together with similar plans and purposes. He who has different plans or purposes is unwelcome.

Geographical communities say that anyone on the other side of the river or tracks cannot belong. It is hard to believe God put rivers on earth to separate men or that the railroad engineer had such a motive.

Personal communities say "No Black, no Orientals, no 'native' Americans" or the like. Boy Scouts demand an age limit, the F.F.A., a rural area, and so on.

Most communities have some kind of a constitution and by-law which spell out quite exactly the requirements for membership. Generally they are put in a positive manner for inclusion, then negatively for exclusion.

Even a young man and woman planning marriage, and consequently a community, include and exclude, albeit unintentionally. "Don't you ever bring friends like him to our house." Or, "She just isn't our type, is she?" Worse yet, in reference to their own future children: "All our children will be intelligent, beautiful, obedient, etc.," implying that any other kind of child would be most unwelcome.

Communities planned by men exclude. The community planned by the God-man, Christ, is all inclusive. He told his Asiatic Hebrew followers to "Go, make disciples of all people." Let us strive to develop the Christian community where all belong.

Today: I will exclude no one from my life for today. How hurting it can be to be excluded. That's what Christians sometimes do—exclude other creatures of God.

When I think about it, I wonder how I can justify passing judgment on anyone! Some day—maybe soon— God will pass judgment upon me. Then what? I wonder what eternity is like?

Attention! At Ease!

Parents, somehow that child of yours is going to get attention. The "how" is up to you unless you leave it up to the child.

It seems that both the parents and the child would prefer attention that is pleasant, affirmative, rewarding, beautiful, deserved and appreciated.

The fact is that all attention is likely to be deserved and appreciated even if it isn't pleasant, affirmative and beautiful.

If the child is praised and complimented for acts which are approved, his efforts will generally increase along those same lines. If approved actions fail, the child soon learns that unapproved actions will not fail in getting proper notice—unless the parents lack all interest whatsoever.

One need not be a genius to discover the three reactions parents can have toward the offspring's action: approval, disapproval or ignoring. The first is great, the second unfortunate, the third inhuman.

If a child can do nothing for approval he generally can find something worthy of disapproval. He will do anything within his power to escape being ignored, regardless of the pain it may cause him. No pain is so great as being unnoticed by someone who has an obligation from God to love you!

Parents, the attention your child wants is by far the easiest to give—easier on you and easier on him. (Parents: Please show this to your children so they can post it in a prominent place for the well-being of everyone's nervous system.)

Today: Someday God will either approve or disapprove of me, but He will never ignore me. Human beings may ignore me, but never God. That could be good or bad, but it is a fact. I am so important to God that no day goes unnoticed by Him. The least I can do is treat children as God treats me—take notice. Today I will examine my attitude to any children I may meet. In God's eyes, we are all children. What a privilege—to be a child of God!!

Depends on How You Look at It

A plaque that has become somewhat in evidence, if not popular, states very simply: "The most difficult decision in life is when to start middle age."

There seems to be little question that youth ceases when one stops growing on both ends and starts from the middle, but most Americans refuse to believe that this is the herald for middle age.

Actually middle age is not a thing begun by choice. In fact, we find that others are more capable than ourselves at knowing the moment. When our friends quit telling us we are "good looking" and are happy we are "looking good," we've reached middle age.

Old age is not something to be feared. It is a privilege which is generally accorded to Americans more than anyone else. Yet, we are generally least prepared for it. There is only one alternative to old age—I'm not sure if we are any better prepared for that.

Perhaps the so-called generation gap makes middle age and old age even less attractive—and confusing, since the young dye the hair grey and the old dye it "natural."

The real problem with growing old is that in fearing the possibility it seems quite impossible to do it gracefully. Fear doesn't allow us to do anything gracefully.

If we put more emphasis on the possibility of growing full of grace we would surely grow old gracefully. And really, isn't it true? It is easier to tell someone they are looking good than that they are good looking.

Today: What about those who can't decide whether to dye the hair grey or natural? Maybe that's why there are so many grey-haired blondes or so many streaked black heads. It seems difficult to remain a child, yet more difficult to face senility. We're such peculiar beings—we never know what we want. To be full of grace is to be graceful, whether it's a child or an adult.

Today I'll examine my state of grace. Maybe I can become more full of grace. Hail Mary, full of grace, help fill me with grace.

Goodness

Man, every man, wants to do good. Only God can read the individual's heart accurately—man can easily deceive himself.

When one reads the works of Karl Marx he sees first of all that he is doing his very best to give right answers to the world's problems and secondly, with no help from God.

The same conclusions come in reading the book of Adolph Hitler. Like many historical figures he assumed the role of savior—if not for the world, at least for the German people. Again, however, there was little room for Christ.

Few of us pretend we can change the world. Most of us feel incapable of changing the small world of everyday life in which we find ourselves. Unfortunately, we don't always feel capable of changing ourselves.

Perhaps this is the key to human failure: that we try to change ourselves as Marx did the world and Hitler did to Germany. Such an attempt at change without any reference to Christ is disastrous to the world, the nation, or the individual.

Man's intrinsic desire to do good for himself and others can find little success if such a desire remains only on the natural level. Since Christ allows us the supernatural dimension of living we have no right to be less as Christians.

"With me you can do all things: without me you can do nothing." The message is as clear as the failures we have had without Him.

Today: Goodness! Goodness!! Goodness!! What is that? Just what is goodness? I think it is something I want. I hope it is something I have. Maybe it is something I should give away. Even the word *goodness* can become confusing. I have a hunch that if I have some—I still want some more. How could I tell if I have goodness? I'm not going to worry about it, lest I lose the little I have. I'm going to trust God that I have "goodness" of heart and that I'm getting more.

Marry-go-round

One of the impossible tasks often confronting the priest is "talking someone out of getting married." The saying, "Love is blind," must have originated in the mind of some clergyman after such a frustrating situation.

No matter how bad the prospects are for a happy marriage the eager couple can always point to someone who was younger, poorer, less educated, less prepared—and they are really happy!

Bishop Sheen once said that "Puppy love leads to a dog's life," and it seems too many people think being collared is a blessing.

Marriage may be a maturing process but it is a process for the mature. Anyone who thinks marriage is an escape from all his problems will generally one day wish he had only the old problems to escape.

One has an obligation to self, to spouse, to children and society to bring into marriage the best possible, most complete person one can be. To do less is, somehow, perpetrating a fraud.

Too many people are ready to marry who aren't ready for marriage. This has to be the obvious conclusion when one realizes that 41% of marriages in America end in divorce.

Wouldn't it be a wonderful change if more people were ready for marriage instead of so many anxious to marry?

Today: Since I don't know much about being ready for marriage I'll sit back and pray for those who are either married or are preparing for marriage. I never could figure out how a woman can live a whole lifetime with one man—even the same man. It takes perseverance to marry! God bless the married. On the other hand—God bless us celibates too, lest we put our hand to the plough and look back.

Follow Me

Americans have always been mission minded. Perhaps this is true because we have always had a great admiration for the pioneer spirit.

The pioneers forged new trails amidst new trials. Even though life was dull there always existed the possible and probable thrill of new discovery.

The image of the pioneer was one of rugged singularity and spirited individualism. He was often a law unto himself. If he followed any laws, they were the forces of nature.

He needed fresh air and much room. When neighbors moved in, he moved on. There was always the other side of the river or mountain to offer him sanctuary.

Today the missions are not across oceans or continents. They are in the inner city, in the classroom, in the theater, everywhere man is.

The pioneer is now the person who is willing to be first—as he has always been. Someone must begin saying hello to the new neighbor, to help the widow in the block, to establish peace by a hearty handshake.

Today's pioneer no longer can escape an undesirable society. He must change it. And he changes it by humbly accepting change within himself, lest he be a blind man leading the blind.

The time of the pioneer and missionary is not in the past. It is in the present—if we accept the challenge. We can no longer move out to be alone. We must move in and be neighborly.

Today: Today is Valentine's Day. I love it. I remember my first dozen roses on a Valentine's Day. I remember those large, heart shaped chocolate boxes. Valentine's Day is for Catholics too. It's a yearly reminder that we all have one thing in common—personal relationships.

Friendship is a relationship wherein persons give of themselves to one another. Valentine's Day reminds us of it. There is no greater love than this, to lay down one's life for one's friends.

How does Jesus want me to express giving love? Trying to answer that will keep me busy all this day. I better get started. Night comes so quickly.

The Thing is the Play

The spirit of the seventies is "Let me do my thing! Accept me as I am!" Quite often the person who insists he does "his thing" has nothing to do, and if he is going to be accepted it will be as he is because the odds are the only change will be added years.

If teachers allow the students to do their thing, we can turn all our school rooms into kindergartens.

If every twelve year old were allowed to drive the family car as he would wish, we might not have very many thirteen year olds.

Simon Peter would have remained an unknown fisherman if Christ had allowed the first pope to do his thing.

The Christian spirit demands that a person be accepted as he is—but not allowed to remain there. Each Christian friendship demands a new birth, an intense growth and a fierce will to improve life in particular and in general.

The Christian "thing" is the acceptance of every person as one created in God's image, a brother or sister in Christ, one capable of being filled with the spirit.

Such an acceptance is the entering into the threshold by each person into the community of the three persons of God.

Can a Christian be less than a Christian once he understands the importance of being a person in the Christian Community? "Let me do my thing" eventually must change to "let me do Christ's thing."

Today: The words "my thing" and "community" seem to contradict each other. It's like *mine* within a family. I wonder how many family squabbles started over the word *mine*—my ball, my sucker, my balloon, my electric train, my car, my room, my inheritance.

Wonder what needs changing in my life regarding the use of *me* and *mine*? Another day's work ahead. It might take me all day to figure it out, but if I ever get the answer, I'll be able to help others—even if I'm old, or sick, or crippled. There's no rest for those who still breathe God's air.

Why Not Change?

We are generally led to believe that security and change cannot exist at the same time. Strangely enough, this concept is quite false since change is necessary for real security.

Parents are usually convinced they offer their children the greatest security. The child accepts this as a fact during his early years. Then suddenly he "rejects" home security for the outside world and its influences.

The initial reaction of the parents is often one of frustration: "Why can't you stay home once in awhile? Why must you always be running off?" The youngster finds this an embarrassing question which is answered generally in an emotional outburst rather than a convincing reason: "No one my age ever stays home. What is there to do around here?"

Such questions and answers are normal procedure. If the teenager would sit at home all the time, watching television, reading books or whatever, the parents would be very upset after a short period of time: "Don't you have any friends? Don't you get tired of sitting all day watching TV?"

Any child who finds his only security at home is really insecure. He doesn't forego the security of home by broadening or changing his interests.

A man who is secure is not afraid of change. A person who fears change has no security—or his security is neither well founded nor grounded.

Pope John the Twenty Third as our supreme pontiff was the symbol of security as pope—but he is referred to as the "pope of change." Let us be secure in our hope for change—let us pray that changes will all be for our happiness.

Today: Why do people sometimes answer questions with an emotional outburst? My dad would have said it is adolescent. Mom would have said it's kiddish and childish. Adults sometimes do it, though. They answer others emotionally. That could be good or it could be evil. But then, someone once defined adolescence as being like a mid-air passage from one trapeze bar to another. By that definition most adults would be adolescent. I am, because sometimes I move emotionally from one trapeze to another. Why can life be so difficult yet so beautiful? That's my mental challenge for today— trying to think about that.

Blindness

A young man had the great misfortune of losing his eyesight as the result of an accident. He was a man of means and went to several specialists, none of whom could help him.

Eventually, he was without funds. He prevailed upon a very close friend, borrowed money, learned to type and began to write his autobiography.

Night and day, since it made no difference to him, he worked. After several months, he was finished. With great enthusiasm, he called his friend to read what he hoped might eventually sell so he could approach more specialists on his blindness.

He handed his manuscript to his friend and waited eagerly for the reaction. There was a quick flipping of papers—a silence. Then the blind man felt the hands of his friend on his shoulders. The strength of the hands made him weak. They were hands of support rather than congratulations.

He sat in utter disbelief as he heard the words: "My friend, this is hard to say, but you have been typing with a ribbon that has no ink."

It is well for us to consider our own autobiography. Is our existence such that our book of life is without words? Or to put it more exactly, "Is our life without the Word?"

What a tragedy to merely exist when every Christian has been called to live, to fill his book! We are people of means with the Specialist to fill each chapter, each verse, each sentence with meaning.

Today: What a tragedy—to type with a ribbon that has no ink. It's a greater tragedy to live a life that has no meaning. Why are some lives wasted lives?

Men and women are called by God to grow, to create, to love and to be responsible stewards. Men are called to subdue the earth. That includes subduing myself—even when I feel caged up—or stretched on a bed—or in an overstuffed rocking chair.

To live a day without growing, creating, loving is like typing without a ribbon. I'm not going to type without a ribbon today. I don't have that kind of time left to waste.

Account Balancing

The other day a woman told me an interesting story about her twelve-year-old son. It seems he had considered his status in life and thought it was time for a change—especially his financial status.

As he left for school one morning, he handed his mother a sealed envelope. She opened it and read the contents: Mowing the lawn, 50¢. Trip to the grocer, 25¢. Washing windows, 5¢ each. Shovelling the walks, 50¢. The driveway, $1.00. Other various tasks, discuss and bargain.

That night, on his pillow, she placed his list. Next to it she wrote this: Hospitalization inconvenience when you were born. Frequent change of diapers and preparation of bottle. Make beds daily. Prepare three meals daily. Regular negotiations with your father on your behalf. Washing and ironing, at least weekly. Driving you to school when you oversleep. Price—Your Mother's Love!

The next morning, she expected some conversation on the matter at the breakfast table but not a word was said.

He picked up his books, put them under his arm and went out the door. As he left, he pulled an envelope from one of the books and handed it to her.

In the envelope was the same piece of paper he had given her the day before—jobs and costs. However there was an added comment: Paid in full!

Today: "Paid in full"—those words always look so good in print.

What about reality? Can a person ever pay another in full??

Do weight watchers ever pay each other in full for their support? Do human beings, husbands and wives, children and friends pay in full?

Today I'm going to draw up a list of my unpaid "personal relationship" debts. I might have to go way back to my childhood and recall the fights I had with my brothers and sisters. I fought, yet they never dropped me from the payroll of their love. I have some unpaid love debts. Today I pay up.

Identity

It has become fashionable to be negative. Gradually we are eliminating the positive. At first glance this would make life much easier because it is always easier to destroy than it is to build. In the long run, however, nothing remains except an intolerable existence.

In less than a generation we have allowed ourselves to move from the position of being proud of our American heritage to being ashamed. The national virtues are ignored while the vices are blown way out of proportion.

The same thing is true of our faith. We judge too often the teachings of Christ by man's, and generally few men's failure to abide with them, rather than the beautiful world we would have if all would abide with His way for us.

If the nation and religion which is ours is as bad as some would have us believe, then the future is mighty hard to face. If we accept a bleak future, we must indeed be pessimists.

When a man is convinced that the past is bad, and the future is bleak, the present cannot be a moment of greatness.

Is it any wonder so many people are facing an identity crisis when they consider their nationality a tragedy, their "faith" untenable, and the moment unbearable.

These people must envy anyone who is proud of his nation, devoted to the cause of Christ, and appreciative for each moment of existence—for such a man lives the Scriptural injunction—"Know thyself."

Today: People used to sing "accentuate the positive" but that was a song. Are songs for real? Today I'm going to examine the words of some songs and lyrics.

—This is my commandment

—Yahweh called me

—What the world needs now

Are songs just words for dreamers and poets? Are they for real? Why do people sing one thing and live another? We sing about love and peace, about joy and truth. Yet some people live in hate, sadness and falsehood.

Today I'll try to find one song that really fits me—just me. My chorus might be Tradition.

Concerned

Over a year ago I received the following announcement of joy and concern from a Newman alumna. Recently, I came across it in my files and sent a letter asking permission to have it published.

"Our second child, Mary Elizabeth, was born on January 21, 1969, at 6:05 p.m. and weighed 6 lbs. 6 oz.

"Immediately after birth our doctor voiced concern about Mary's appearance and within a few hours we were informed that we were parents of a special baby. Mary is naturally special to us because she is ours, but she is extra special because she is a mongoloid. For this reason she will have a limited capacity to learn and God may take her away from us before she is very old.

"The chances of a child like Mary being born to parents as young as we, are very slim, and yet God saw fit to send Mary to us. We do not understand God's will, but we do accept it and we pray that Mary's stay with us will be filled with an abundance of love and happiness.

"Please pray for us that we may have the courage to face an uncertain future with knowledge and strength to be understanding and patient."

In this time when so many persons are so disinterested in life that they are willing to terminate it before it can be shared, it is very refreshing to hear from citizens so concerned for life.

Today: We've all heard the words stated, "The glory of God is man fully alive." Maybe that's why some people practice abortion. Maybe they don't believe in God. Maybe they don't want God to have the glory of another man, *fully alive*. The statement seems true. The ideal sounds beautiful to me. To really understand it, we'd have to answer some other questions first. What does it mean to parents to have children fully alive? How do they get children fully alive? Abortion and life—such complex thoughts.

Today I'm going to try to figure out how the aged and sick can still be fully alive lest someone practice euthanasia on me!!!

To Life

An unwillingness to be crucified is a failure to taste life. It is difficult to say, "Mom, I love you," if one is afraid she might answer, "So what?"

Too often a person refuses to run for an office, not because he considers himself unqualified but because he hates to face the embarrassment of being defeated.

It is easier to bear no fruit than have people throwing sticks at you to knock the apples from the branches.

The person who is told to 'mind his own business' very seldom has one other than interfering with another's.

Life is full of contradictions. It is easier to fault a professional quarterback for a single mistake than it is to instruct the beginner as to how to handle the ball. The dent, be it small, in a newly polished car is much more obvious than an entire auto ready to fall apart at the next bump.

We toss and turn over a single failure whereas we sleep contentedly with success even though our efforts may have been much greater in defeat. The incorrect answer is remembered long after the accurate answers are forgotten.

Let us not be so concerned about the first dent that we hesitate to leave the garage. Let us not be so afraid of making mistakes that we do nothing. Let us be doers of the word.

If we are of Christ we must have a willingness to be crucified—to taste life.

Today: My dad told me once that the one way I could be sure I would not break cups was not to wipe dishes. What he was really trying to tell me, I think, was that when we are willing to stick our neck out, we might get stuck. People who stick out their necks, are liable to make mistakes. They are liable to be hurt. What's the alternative? Pray for courage!

That's what I'll do today. I'll pray for courage to stick my neck out when I should. A person really has to care to stick their neck out. Lord, help me stick my neck out.

Now

Since the Church was founded, we have had some Christians whose main concern is the Second Coming of Christ. They form groups and sects and await the terrible end of the present structures and a thousand years of joy.

The unfortunate aspect of such anticipation is that all things worthwhile are in the future and only contempt can be had for the present. It constitutes a psychological suicide in an unhappy morbid now.

Yet, the Scriptures tell us that "now" is a good time. "Now" is the moment of salvation. "Now" is the time to arise from sleep.

Christ's first coming was the moment of joy at Christmas when He proceeded from the womb of the Virgin Mary. His Second Coming was the moment He came forth from the tomb of the earth on Easter Sunday.

If the Second Coming is not "now," then Christ has deceived us since He told his disciples He "will be with you all days even to the end of the world."

Hence, it is not the end of the world we point to as Christians in awaiting the Christ. He is with us now. The millennium of joy will begin the moment the world accepts the living Christ in word and in deed.

Christ has already conquered sin and death. If we are concerned over either it is because we have not accepted Him or His teachings and we have no part with Him.

Christ is life. Life is sacrament. It is our responsibility to accept Christ, life and sacrament. Today, now, is the moment we celebrate the Second Coming.

Today: Everybody wants to be a NOW person. Come to think of it, St. John the Baptist did say, "Now is the acceptable time." "*Now* is the hour of salvation."

Today I'll examine some NOW moments in my life.

What is the state of my spiritual life NOW? What is my relationship with the Church NOW? Am I ready to die NOW? Can I say to everyone, "Peace be with you NOW" or "I forgive you NOW"?

My day might be a different one if I live my moments well. I'll give it a try for today. Tomorrow may call for a repeat performance.

Like Man!

In recent times we constantly are having our consciences awakened to world problems. The Church stands as a sign of hope not just in pointing out the problems but also the solutions to those problems.

The Church is not a perfect society demanding conformity but rather a community moving continually toward God.

The call to be holy is the call to be human. The Son of God became man to impress mankind with its own intrinsic worth. To be less than human, or inhuman, is to reject what Christ accepted for Himself.

Man's inhumanity to man was experienced completely by the Savior on the cross so that none of us should ever inflict further damage on any brother.

The Church teaches us that any Sacrament in which we participate is a participation in the life of Christ. Consequently life is sacrament if we live up to our human potential.

We cannot be more than human and as Christians we cannot be less than human. If the Son of God considered it not beneath his dignity to be one with us then we must strive to be one with Him in the sacrament of life.

Saint Paul sums it up very succinctly when he says, "For me to live is Christ!" Acceptance of this concept by all men is the only answer to the problems facing humanity.

Today: If all men faced the problems of humanity, then what? Would we all be out demonstrating for peace? Would we all be out working for reconciliation with one another? How can I reorganize my thinking so that for me "to live is Christ"?

The song words say, "Let there be peace on earth, and let it begin with me." An important demonstration or celebration for peace is now called the *Rite of Reconciliation*. It's in the Sacrament of Peace where members of the Catholic Community are united with Jesus—in peace. Jesus said, "I no longer call you servants but friends." (John 15:15)

Balance

There seems to be a constant struggle between stability and change. The young generally demand change, the old search for stability. The not so obvious is that our nature demands both.

In the past the Church offered stability. Every Catholic possessed a comfortable, undisturbed piety. There was no searching but merely an acceptance of teachings without question or doubt.

Suddenly change came into the Church, and with change, crisis. In any situation of crisis there arises a creativity in the human soul— and with creativity comes a better world. Change which excludes Christ is destructive. Change with Christ is creative.

People of faith must be open to truth regardless of its source. We are interested in the past, present and future. The Christian has confidence in the ultimate. There must be a constant hope in doctrinal development and a language development which will aid understanding and acceptance of doctrine.

If we settle for stability only we negate our freedom of searching for deeper truths. If we hunger for change only we endanger the responsibility we have toward truths already possessed.

The modern Church is demanding of each member that he remain free and responsible. Anyone who is free and responsible can rejoice with change and stability.

Freedom and responsibility so often seem at odds but only when maturity is lacking. There is no discord when a free person is responsible or when responsible people are free.

Today: Church, change, crisis, council all begin with the letter c. So do the words Christ, confession, conscience and courage. I wonder if that is supposed to mean something. It could!!

The Church Council required change that caused crisis. Christ asks us to examine our conscience and confess our sins with courage. That's enough to think about for today—crisis—Christ—courage and change. It's almost exciting.

Truth is Truth

One of the criticisms against the teachings of Christianity is that the same teachings are very often found in pagan religions pre-dating Christ.

To say that Christ's teachings are, in part, found elsewhere, does not necessarily indicate He borrowed—nor need we assume He did not.

The fact is, the truth is the truth regardless of its source. The devil quoting Scripture does not void Scripture. It makes Scripture neither better nor worse. It is still the word of God.

Similarly, what Jesus teaches must be acceptable to the Christian whether the teaching was original with Him or not.

The catholicity, or universality of the Church, demands teaching that can be accepted by all peoples at all times. Similarities between Christian doctrine and other teachings is merely a further argument as to its soundness.

It is easier to teach the way of Christ to the neophyte if he sees in the teachings not just what is reasonable—but more importantly something he can associate with that which he holds already true and acceptable.

Truth is truth regardless of its source. If we reject truth because of its source we are fools indeed—just as foolish as to accept error because we love the source!

In Christ, however, the question is resolved since He is the source and the truth. "I am the way, the light and the *truth*," He said of Himself.

Today: If truth is truth regardless of the source then falsehood is false regardless of the source. Is that good logic? Sometimes people say, "Well, just consider the source." Does the source of something change the reality? If the source of my pain is cancerous tissue or rheumatoid joints, is it still real pain? Is pain, pain regardless of the source just like truth is truth regardless of the source? Is love really love, regardless of the source? Is peace always peace, regardless of the source?

Guess this will require some thought today.

Mom's the Word

One gets the feeling sometimes that mothers are fast becoming extinct. One isn't sure whether we should put them in zoos as oddities for the sake of preservation or just give up on mothers as a lost cause.

For the time being I think we should let them decide for themselves whether they prefer the love of children or something else might be more wonderful—whether anything can ever be given that is more important than life.

Mother's Day is sort of celebrating one's own birthday and existence except it is even better since one has the chance to give instead of receive.

This is a very special opportunity to return thanks to the one who co-created with God one's own being.

If the Son of God wanted to rest nine months next to the heart of Mary it would seem that any woman honoring that Son would rejoice in carrying His brother or sister near and dear to her own heart.

This is a day, too, that we forget and forgive Mother's failures. So she stuck you with a safety pin, by accident—but it was your fault she needed to change the diapers.

God bless you Mothers—and Dads, there is a special grace to say before dinner today and often: "May God bless this food and the devoted person who prepared it."

Today: Calm, peace and joy! That's what I remember about my mom. Without her, I wouldn't be alive. That goes for all of us. Without a mom, we just wouldn't be. Mothers, usually, are persons we respect and admire. What they are rubs off, in part, on their children. In fact, it rubs off on all who come in contact with them. So, mothers, beware! What you are, others will become. I guess that deserves a special prayer today. God bless all mothers.

To Where?

Some time ago a clergyman approached a very wealthy parishioner for some financial aid for a parish need. The man was sympathetic and gave a donation. As the clergyman was leaving he said, "This is very wise of you. After all, if you were to die the government would get the money."

The contributor quickly responded: "Reverend, I don't see any tragedy in that possibility. The government has always been good to me."

Somehow, we have come to think the government owes us everything whether we pay or not. In fact, not paying becomes an annual hope or dream.

The dropout is under the impression that society owes him everything. He resents the very society on which he is totally dependent. It is the nature of a parasite to destroy that on which it feeds even though eventually it means its own destruction.

To be pushed along with every wind is to be battered and bruised—to face the wind and breathe deeply is exhilarating and refreshing. When one lacks direction he has little right to complain about his destination. The ship without a rudder may go far—but 'where' must always be the question.

If the establishment needs a new direction it cannot be given by the dropout. One doesn't abandon ship to save it—nor does an intelligent person abandon ship when his own chances of survival are lessened by so doing.

When each of us assumes our role as loyal citizen and loyal Christian we will have the establishment needed. Anything less is unfortunate.

Today: Each of us brings to society and to the government our own set of values, beliefs, character and even our temperament. The challenge is to figure out how to incorporate "me" into what is the best in the land. It's only when I give my best, that we will get the most perfect direction. As long as anyone fails to give his/her best to society, all of us will be battered and bruised. Just who wants to be responsible for someone else's bruises? The alternative is to give my best—today and everyday.

Together Alone

One of the strangest experiences in many lives is something that happens in music. Generally in choral or orchestral groups one practices first in a rather small room. Under such circumstances he hears the total sound of all participants and his own role is unnoticed by himself. He is part of the din.

Then suddenly the group is moved onto a large stage in a huge auditorium and everything is different. All at once, each person hears himself for the first time. He feels as though he is a soloist and to his alarm he is quite uncertain of himself. It is just as though the responsibility rests suddenly and totally upon him and not the group.

In a sense, all of life is like that. We grow up in the protection of the family. From that, our circle widens to the favorable environs of the classroom. In all one does, he has the advice of parents, teachers, clergymen, counsellors and friends.

Then somewhere, sometime, he has the final graduation. He leaves the cocoon and has to fly alone. In his mind, he is alone. He is a soloist.

Yet, each man must realize that throughout life he is part of the group. He must maintain his individuality but somehow produce notes that will not create discords where harmony is the desired result.

There are times too when a man's conscience tells him the protection of the group is not always in his or its best interest. These are the times in which he may very well have to rise above the din of the crowd and stand by himself—a victim, a hero—or both!

Today: Each one of us is called to grow, to love, to create and to be responsible. There comes a moment for each one of us when we must "let go" and spin our own web—make our own cocoon. Sometimes we may stay suspended in mid-air, but "let go" we must. Anyone who doesn't let go just stays in the same spot.

Sometimes growth is given up for the sake of security. Just who needs that much security? We were born to be free!!

Pentecostals

Much talk has taken place in recent months concerning Pentecostalism. The only neutrals are those unaware of the movement.

Those opposed generally say that the early Church, when still new, had need of the gifts of tongue, prophecy and healing. They say that St. Paul tells us these things will all pass away in favor of charity which never ceases.

I suppose the answer to these objections rests in the fact that if the new Church had these things, it is only fitting that a renewed Church have them also. There is little evidence that the world is filled with charity. Maybe we need the Spirit desperately.

At the first Pentecost, the Apostles spoke so all nations could have understanding. There is no question that ecumenism is more alive today among Pentecostals than anywhere else. It is crossing denominational lines without any evidence of any compromise of doctrine.

My reaction to Pentecostalism is voiced very well in the Acts of the Apostles by Gamaliel when he spoke to the Sanhedrin about Christainity: "If it is of God, we must do nothing to hinder it. If it is merely of man, it will not survive."

No one can question the need of the Spirit. No one should pretend to limit His power or means to act through the Church. "The Spirit is A-Movin."

Today: Pentecost—a time to renew my belief that through the strength of the Holy Spirit, the Church grew and grew and grew.

The same Holy Spirit is with the Church today and always. If I am alive with that Spirit, I will act on behalf of Christ for the good of my family or community. I believe that the Holy Spirit is the source of any spiritual strength I may have. If the Holy Spirit changed frightened, discouraged men into fearless Apostles, then it can happen to me too. My problem is, I'm not always *open to the Spirit*. That's bad!

Frontiersmanship

Most of us, as children or adults, have been told, "You can't have your cake and eat it." At such times we might forget that it was Christ and not Marie Antoinette who said, "Man does not live by bread alone."

It is precisely in the realization that one cannot have his cake and eat it too that the present generation sees the emptiness of materialism. In fact, because the materialism of Communism has provided so little of the material, it actually has an attraction for some intellectuals.

Spiritual values, like material goods, are most appreciated and desired in their absence. Because we are so devoid of things pertaining to the spirit in the Western world, many are turning to the philosophies of the East for answers.

Like any other vacuum, the spiritual vacuum demands filling. Our society must turn to reading and prayer. It has no choice if it wishes survival and improvement.

Just as one cannot eat his cake and have it—just so one *can* digest a book and have it. To use the material is to destroy it. To use the spiritual is to preserve and strengthen it.

A society based on the material brings on its own destruction whereas one with a solid spiritual foundation is capable of a constant re-creation. Consequently society is strengthened or destroyed eventually from within.

We, as Christians, must remember that Society is people. Let us have the inner spiritual strength necessary for an ever needed rebirth.

Today: The fact is, I can't eat my cake and still have it. I can have it for a while and eat it later, but not vice versa. Men came to care most about the beauty and resources of nature as environmentalists warn that we are "running out."

Today I'm going to do a little thinking about how I act toward the world in which I live. We read in the Book of Genesis that God created this world and saw that it was good. Do I make it less fit for human life?

Friend

It is not too often we think of it in these terms, but friendship is an ownership. We find it easy to say, "I have a friend," but difficult to accept, "I own a friend."

A little child can persistently demand attention of the mother. Sometimes it requires tears to get the message across: "You are *my* mother!" It is interesting that the only way the parent can dissuade the child is by admitting: "I am *your* mother, now be quiet while I finish the dishes."

A youngster gets great satisfaction when he hears he has a guardian angel—all to himself. The angel belongs to the child and the child belongs to the angel.

When one wants to terminate a friendship, the quickest way is to merely inform the other person: "You don't own me!"

The joint ownership in marriage is not merely of home and car, it is of one another. I own my hand, it is part of me. In marriage the couple is also one flesh—and one mind and heart.

When Christ chose the Apostles, He merely said, "Come, follow me." They left all they owned. Nets, boats and even fathers were abandoned in favor of owning the friendship of Christ.

Friendship demands a mutual and reciprocal owning. Even Our Lord wants us to own Him as we do in the Eucharist and prayer. That is why Christ's words are so meaningful: "I do not call you servants but friends."

The word "friend" demands a possessive pronoun, my, your, our, their. Friendship is ownership. Isn't it good to belong to Christ?

Today: How can I be "possessed" by my friends yet be "A Man for Others," like Christ and Thomas More? That's a problem. When I turn the thought around, it makes more sense. Jesus Christ possesses me and I possess Jesus, so that I can become that man for others—that man for all seasons. Jesus is never exhausted, even when I am.

Today I'll really take a look at Jesus and see what He presents—ever fresh—ever new.

Dear Dad

I've often thought that you really brought me into a pretty terrible world. And somehow I've held you responsible for its condition. Yet, today, when I prayed for you at Mass, I suddenly realized that you are a terrific man. You love me—and all my friends' dads love them. Who in the world makes this planet such an awful place? Is it all those fellows who don't have kids?

I saw your old report cards in grandma's attic last month. Your marks weren't too good either. Even your effort and conduct marks could have been easily improved. I think you are trying much harder now.

Mom said when I was born you carried me around like I was the last word in the process of human evolution—even though anyone with any vision could see I was made in your "spitting" image.

I get quite upset when you are always doing "this" for my own good. You may mean well but sometimes it is awfully hard to translate until later. On some things I guess I'll have to be as old as you are before I understand why you say "no" to so many reasonable requests.

You've lost a lot of hair since I first remember you. Aunt Mary says I was the main cause for you pulling it out of your head. I wished I dared to write how much I think of you. It would be embarrassing—so I'll just go on thinking you are the greatest dad in existence.

I hope somehow the comb I'm giving you on your day will be a hint as to how much I love you. I wanted to get you much more but my baseball glove cost too much—and I know you'd want me to have a glove . . .

Today: I wonder why so many children are an image of their dad? Could it have something to do with the fact that God, our Heavenly Father, made us to His image and likeness? I really do believe so many of us are in reality "a chip off the old block." But the really important thing is our relationship with dad. I love my dad so much that if he weren't mine, I'd want to adopt him. Today I'm going to pray for all fathers so they'll be concerned more about giving *life* than money to their children.

After all—when my life goes, the money goes too.

Cool It

When I was a child I heard a story which made a great impression on me. A small boy was sitting on the curb crying his eyes out over an obvious disaster. In the gutter was his spilled ice cream cone.

An old man passing by quickly caught the tragedy and walked slowly over to the boy and inquired as to the cause for such tears. The lad blurted out the simple fact that he was suddenly deprived of a favorite food by a lack of attention to his ice cream.

The man stroked his chin slowly and asked the boy to remove his shoes and stockings. The child hesitated for a moment and then slowly took them off.

"Now," said the man, "step on the ice cream and let it ooze up between your toes. Notice how wonderful and cool it is. But above all, realize you are the only boy in town who has ever enjoyed the cooling effect of ice cream squishing through his toes." The lad was delighted.

It isn't easy to make the best of bad situations—and as an adult one can smile over frozen spilled milk—but in comparison, do we have any problems more tragic facing us than the lost ice cream for a little boy?

As we grow we mature according to our ability not to merely accept our crosses but much more importantly to turn them to the sanctification of others and self.

Today: Spilling milk is a part of growing up. Learning not to cry about it or blaming others for the spilling is also a part of growing up. Sometimes it is easy to do the spilling, but not so easy not to cry or lay the blame on someone else. Thank God it isn't *wrong* to cry over spilled milk. It is just immature. In fact, maybe sometimes it is good to cry over the milk I've spilled. At least I'm admitting that I made an error. Have I lost the art of admitting my guilt or my wrongdoing?

I Declare!

There are many examples of actions speaking louder than words, but one of the best is the Declaration of Independence and the Revolutionary War.

Not one single newspaper in all of the British Isles took the "Declaration" seriously. Editorials passed it off as folly and generally asked the government to treat the whole matter with an appropriate sense of humor.

The reaction to the war was one of utter disbelief. Initial successes by the "redcoats" were expected. Newspapers asked for clemency for the colonials—and more than clemency was attained with the turning of the tides of battle.

The War of 1812 was, in a sense, an attempt by the British to see if the conflict of the 70's really had the published facts of defeat and victory. Suddenly, England had lost two wars!

It will never be sufficient to declare freedom. It must be lived—not merely by flying flags, watching fireworks and going on picnics. Nazi Germany had those things, as does Communist Russia.

The important thing is to fly the flag, watch fireworks, and go on picnics when one wants to. No law in America says we must do these things—and many other things which signify freedom.

If freedom rings it is not in the liberty bell but rather in the hearts, minds and bodies of free men.

Today: Am I really free? Are you really free? Freedom is important to people, because it gives them an opportunity to express themselves. It allows one to be who one wants to be. Freedom gives one the ability to be one's own kind of person.

Today I'm going to examine the ways in which I express myself as a unique person. I'll think about the clothes I wear, the choice of friends I've made and most of all the decisions I make.

Memories of the Future

There seems to be a cry in the world today for a new set of virtues. The hint is that the old ones are either outdated or not meaningful.

It is never made clear whether these new virtues would be totally new concepts or just new names for the "old" virtues—or if the new virtues would destroy the need for the ones we presently have.

I suppose if we destroy the sacred mystery of the person there will be no need of faith. If sensitivity sessions remove all inhibition and individuality so that all experience must be common, then faith is a memory.

And if one is deluded into thinking he is God, there is little room left for hope. Hope is expecting the realization of our desires and dreams. If I am divine, then what more can I have for which to hope? Yet, I hope for so much that I cannot be God. Somehow, I need hope even as I want faith.

Love. Generally a couple, in the initial stages of romance, use all sorts of words to signify love: sometimes because they are afraid to express their sentiments totally—sometimes because they think their relationship is stronger than love.

Gradually, if the virtue persists and matures, they come to know there is no stronger word than love to define their total dedication to one another.

Let us not search for new virtues until we have really tried the old ones. Faith, hope and love by any other name are still faith, hope and love.

Today: Everyone faces a crisis now and then. It is at the time of crisis that a person most needs faith, hope and love. So often we hear people say, "This I believe," or "I hope that—," or "I really love it."

Sometimes it is difficult to put into words what we really believe. In that, we are not alone. When we try to verbalize our beliefs, our hopes and our loves, the words seem to be either too few or too many.

Today I will examine the creed we recite every Sunday at Mass. It took three centuries for the Church to formulate that creed. No wonder even I am confused sometimes about my beliefs, my hopes and my loves. Today, I'll make up my own creed.

Light Up

The scripture that forbids us to hide our light under a bushel goes on to say that, "He who has much will receive more. He who has little, will have even that taken from him."

It might seem that Christ is saying, "The rich get richer and the poor get poorer." The Lord who came to bring happiness to the poor isn't interested in followers to the extent that he wants more people in need so He can have more disciples.

Sometimes we are so oblivious of our gifts that we fail to recognize and consequently to use them. If we hide our light so well that even we cannot discover them, then it is only natural that the gift remain under the bushel.

When our gifts and talents are used to the best of our ability they increase and grow. The pianist must practice regularly or his touch is gradually lost. The artist must ply his paints or the canvas becomes the stranger.

Each person, on his own, increases the gifts he has by usage. He who has little in the way of gifts from God generally lacks the vision to recognize the talents and his ability to use them.

"Seek and you shall find," is a promise. He who looks not for a gift stands little chance of finding—even the obvious.

The old bromide, "The Lord helps him who helps himself," is an apt translation for, "Who has much will receive more . . . " And, "What might have been," is translated from, "Who has little will have even that taken from him."

Today: Jesus seems so strong yet so gentle. He had such strong principles, yet was gentle with people. Jesus was so firm when He told us we may not hide our candle (talents) under a bushel basket.

Our aim, then, must be to know our capabilities, to accept them and to thank God for having given us something "to crow about."

Each of us needs to study ourself, to stand up tall and believe in ourselves.

Since I am a special creature, God has given me some talents and He expects me to use them. I better get moving!

Christophers

Most of us, at one time or another, have paused to consider the picture of one boy carrying another—and underneath the caption: "He ain't heavy, he's my brother."

Sometimes, when we carry our brother's weight, it is very heavy indeed. Sometimes, though, it is a heavier load on our persons if we refuse to carry him.

If our brother calls to us when he is in distress and we ask him to wait until we finish our coffee, the beverage suddenly becomes bitter and we wonder if it wouldn't taste better if we tasted it after our return—even though it be cold.

If we are brothers in Christ, it is essential as Christians to "carry" one another's burdens. Christ accepted us as his brothers by carrying His cross, our cross, to Calvary.

There is a tendency at times to ignore the fact that we have an obligation to carry our number one brother, Christ, wherever we go. Even though he guarantees his burden is sweet and his yoke is light we easily persuade ourselves to the contrary.

How do we carry Christ? How do we act as His brothers? He tells us very simply "Whoever does the will of God is brother, and sister and mother to me."

Today: People sitting next to each other at a ballgame show emotion and excitement, but do they share each other's burden? How much do they even share their blanket on a cold day at a football game?

Do people who have never seen each other before and will never see each other again really share each other's burdens? Why are we so unwilling to build up passing relationships except at sports' events or at traffic accidents?

Members of a "Weight-watchers" group help carry each other's burdens. I doubt, though, that Christ meant us to stop at that. Today I will share someone else's burden.

Togetherness

When Christ sent his disciples to teach all nations, He admonished them to keep certain rules: "Go two by two, take no extra money, no extra tunic and take only one pair of sandals."

At first glance He seems to be stressing the necessity of poverty for His followers. When we look at our wardrobe we have to admit that we really don't qualify as disciples if we have such full closets.

After further perusal, I think we can easily miss the main point of Christ's admonition. He is telling us not to put too much emphasis on the material things in the world.

If we have but one body, we can wear only one pair of sandals at a time. The second tunic would at best be clumsy. And the necessary food for daily existence doesn't demand a fortune.

I think what Our Lord is saying is that we must have friends—good friends, who know us well enough so we can communicate in silence. A friend who can be more than another self because he knows us better than we know ourselves.

Christ put things in proper order. He didn't first stress the notion of poverty but rather the real wealth this world has to offer—the wealth of friendship! "Go two by two."

Without friendship the work of Christ remains undone. In friendship His labors are performed, His teachings learned, His love shared. Lack of clothing and money is understandable. Lack of friendship is not.

Today: How does Jesus want us to express friendship? Jesus knew what it meant to give love to His friends. Friendship always involves giving and receiving. Friends don't just give things and ideas. They give real love. Only those relationships in which persons give of themselves and receive what others have to offer can be called friendships.

Today I will spend some time thinking about the relationships I have in my life. Some are permanent, some are just casual. But in all I want to be able to say, "As the Father has loved me, so have I loved you." That's real love.

Wait

There is a great lesson to be learned at wakes. When people gather to pay their last respects they are filled with charity.

It is easy to conclude that this is the case because the convened are all friends. The fact is that one seldom hears anything unkind about the dead.

Why? Is it because death solves all problems? Is it because the dead cannot defend themselves? Is it because the dead can no longer perform evil acts and hence all can be forgotten as ancient history?

I don't think any of these answers is adequate. But the answer is available. First, the deceased is facing a more just judge than ourselves and our judgments are foolishness.

Secondly, in death, a person is preparing to make amends for a total life. Whatever in the past stands before him, he asks forgiveness and mercy more sincerely than ever before.

Thirdly, we suddenly realize how unfair it is to judge anything until we see the finished product. Not until man dies is his life complete. In death a man's past folly suddenly makes sense. His most logical actions suddenly become folly.

Total life is seen most easily in death. Until that moment we don't have totals that are accurate. Perhaps we might do well to put off our judgments of our fellow man till the totals are in—better for us, better for our fellow man!

Today: No man is an island—not even while his coffin is still open. If none of us is an island, then we ought to be a community of people who can share each other's joys and pains. Just why don't people enjoy each other's dignity and beauty?

Each person I meet has the potential of becoming more a person because of me. That puts quite a responsibility upon me.

Today I'll give that some thought. I'll try to realize the power of one telephone call, one letter or one short visit.

It's too late when someone is dead. Then I have only my regret to live with.

Hail Mary

Unless Christ is man He cannot identify with and atone for the human race. Since God is His father, it is obvious that He is one with us only if His mother is truly and completely human.

To presume that she is in any way more than human is as wrong as to presume she is less than human. We speak as children of Adam and Eve when we address her as our mother. We speak as children of God when we address Christ as our brother.

Since Mary is our mother and the mother of Christ, she is the essential person in God's plan for the restoration of mankind as His kind. Without Mary, Christ would be truly God and only God.

Sometimes Catholics are accused of giving Mary too much honor. This accusation is foolishness since no one can honor her more than God has when He chose her as His mother. Our honoring Mary is merely a faint reflection of Christ giving her His total person.

If Christians have thought it good to honor His cross, His birth place, His burial place—how much more logical to honor, as the Scripture says, "The womb that bore him and the breasts that nursed Him"—as well as the one total person who "heard His word and kept it" with a total motherly love and dedication.

How foolish to think one can love the Son and not honor the source. Today, in a very special way, we in the Catholic Church celebrate the reunion of Christ and His mother. We honor her less than Christ honors her because we are only human—but we honor her especially because she is the source of His human nature.

Today: Where does one look to find the answers to some questions? So often Catholics say, "we look for the resurrection of the dead, and the life of the world to come." That includes seeing Mary, the Mother of Jesus. Most of us don't have answers to our questions about Mary. Maybe it is because we don't look in the right place for the answers. If it is true that, "As the Mother, so the Son," then I ought to look to Jesus for answers about Mary. I wonder how much like Mary Jesus really was. Did they have similiar attitudes, feelings, and fears? Was Jesus her Way, her Truth and her Life too?? Is He mine? Really?

Too Often a Bridesmaid

One of the big problems in life is the possibility of confusing conviction and truth. Conviction is how we see it—truth is how it is. The difficulty is that we think everything as we see it is how it really is.

Sometimes when a person acts with conviction he ends up convinced he made a mistake. The tragic thing is that quite often one has the truth and would rather not act on it.

Conviction and truth should always form a happy marriage but sometimes prejudice refuses an introduction and they never get together.

We are living in an age when repetition of a conviction allows it to look like a truth. And if repetition doesn't suffice, then shouting it loud enough makes all argument ridiculous.

Conviction and truth are generally about as far apart as the mouth and the brain. What man speaks is not thereby necessarily the truth, nor is the truth always demanding a voice—and if it does it can so easily be stifled.

Christ said He was "The way, the truth and the light." We, as Christians, accept this truth but we aren't always convinced enough to live or speak Christ. In fact, we find an uneasy, uncomfortable comfort in silencing the truth of Christ in the world.

It is time to meet the situations of life with an open mind rather than an open mouth. As followers of Christ we must never settle for convictions instead of truth. Let the marriage take place. Let us bring truth and conviction together. Let us be the witnesses.

Today: Each time I express myself, I use my freedom to make a decision. That, to some degree, involves both conviction and truth. My problem is that sometimes I form convictions before I know the whole truth. Freedom to decide, freedom to form one's own convictions, is really one of man's greatest gifts. It calls for maturity—for a sense of responsibility.

Pray, God, I'm mature enough. Better give it a little thought, though. I don't want to take anything for granted.

Silent Generation

He said he had been raised differently. His parents didn't have to give a dozen reasons why he should be obedient. One reason was sufficient and it was always the same reason: "Because I said so."

"Yes," he, number two, said, "we weren't as smart as the kids are today. They have television and educational movies and better schooling. We were all pretty stupid."

He, number one, disagreed: "We weren't so dumb. We were just obedient because we weren't as able to express ourselves. The young people today aren't any smarter than we were. They just know how to speak up."

"That is true," responded number two he, "but we didn't dare open our mouths even when we knew we were right. I always used to wish my dad would wear suspenders instead of a belt. Seems like he had that belt off as soon as I opened my mouth."

"Man, you said it," said number one he. "The main thing we learned as children was to listen. And it's a good thing we learned our lesson so well. It has saved me a lot of arguments with my wife and really has helped keep the family together."

"It is a good thing indeed. My youngsters are really vocal. They are real capable of telling me their wants and needs. And when they aren't talking the music is on too loud for a decent conversation anyway."

"You know, I'm kind of glad your power mower ran out of gas. It isn't often we get to talk. We listened to our parents, we listen to our kids. Now that we have you all refueled we better start the mowers and get back to work. Good talking with you."

Today: Life is full of the "silent generation" people. Most of them also qualify as the "searching generation." People seem to be searching for one thing or another. Some are searching for meaning in life — some are searching for the Lost Chord. Everyone of us searches for what best satisfies our needs. It seems as if the silent people do the best job of searching.

Maybe it isn't such a bad thing after all that we are the "silent generation." Silence does not mean oppression. Silent people are "God influenced."

Excuse vs Reason

What is there that allows one to determine his entire religious outlook on one singular event in his life? So often a person will say he left the Church because a priest said something he didn't like to hear in a sermon. The sermon could have been twenty years earlier when the child was ten, but all his religion crumbles with one incident.

It is presumed of course that the priest, or maybe the parent, was all wrong in speaking to the child. A hundred good sermons are beside the point.

Dozens of kindnesses are easily forgotten. The "Church" has had it because of an erring priest—even though the priest is never allowed to know his "mistake."

If a single incident can destroy the faith of an individual then perhaps one may protest that there isn't much faith to be destroyed. A man of faith is not swayed by adversity but rather has a growth of faith in his searching for solutions.

Man doesn't quit education because of one poor teacher or one bad class. The normal person doesn't quit dating because of one upsetting date. The prospector doesn't expect to find gold on his first attempt— or maybe ever, but his search continues.

Isn't it strange that a man who spends his life in education is honored, the great lawyer is respected, the doctor of medicine is heard, but if one is constant in his faith, he is a fanatic.

Perhaps the problem is a certain lack of honesty. One good religious experience doesn't secure us in a life for Christ—why should one bad experience destroy our life in Him who is Life? Any love demands constancy—why not the love of man for God?

Today: Life within the Church—any Church—is interesting. One can always blame the clergy for whatever goes wrong, or what one doesn't like. I bet they did the same thing in the early Christian Church. I wonder how many people left the Church because Peter or Paul said what they didn't want to hear. Maybe Peter was only popular because people believed in magic.

Today I'm going to examine my approach to the Church as opposed to my approach to the clergy. After all, the clergy really aren't the whole Church.

Love, the Christian Treaty

In Old Testament times there were two kinds of treaties: the parity and suzerainty. The first was an agreement between equals. The second an agreement between a weaker and a stronger party.

The Ten Commandments was an example of the latter. God promised protection for His Chosen People on the condition they would follow His laws. As long as they were obedient He assumed full responsibility for their welfare. If they failed they were on their own.

Before the fall of Adam, man was in the image and likeness of God and the Creator accepted them by "walking and talking" with them in the Garden. Yet there was an agreement to obedience which man broke and lost friendship and protection.

When the Son of God chose to become man He re-established an "equality." He asked that man would become one with Him as He was with the Father.

The new commandment was one of love—love of God and a "same" commandment of loving one's neighbor. Christ requests an attempt by each of us to be perfect as His heavenly Father is perfect.

St. Paul says to owe no man anything except to love one another. This is merely rephrasing Christ except to make love a Christian obligation. Now we owe love in justice!

Christ came to restore all things. All things can be restored only by the fulfillment of the new commandment or treaty of love. It is a good God who demands all things in one word: Love.

Isn't it interesting that John tells us God is Love. Christianity is God's and man's attempt at parity!

Today: A friend that you have to buy isn't worth what you pay for him. I don't know where the idea of parity fits in with the idea of friendship. I suspect it doesn't. Jesus is a true friend, and true friends are gifts of God. I don't think real friends worry much about parity. God forbid that they do. Anyway, St. Paul urged us to love one another and he didn't say anything about parity.

It's hard enough sometimes to love others without finding a fancy name for it.

Reflected Glory

All things reflect the glory of God. When Noah's Ark had settled on the land, God sent a rainbow as a covenant to man indicating He would never again destroy the world with water.

The rainbow contains all colors. It reaches across the sky to remind man of God's goodness. The rainbow demands light. Indeed, as we well know, color is a reflection of the light.

It is interesting that darkness and sin are often equated in Scripture. Sin is a rejection of God's goodness—a situation in which man is totally absorbed in his own pride.

Darkness is the refusal to reflect color. Sin is the refusal to reflect the glory of our Creator, Redeemer and Sanctifier. The rainbow and darkness do not co-exist.

Fairytales and songs portray men as always chasing rainbows. At the end of the rainbow one finds riches and happiness. All darkness, all evil is dispelled. Yet one can never reach the rainbow. It always moves ahead of one, unattainable.

Sometimes we see the rainbow touching another person, just as another can see the rainbow touching us. So often we need other people to remind us that we are living in God's grace, that we do reflect His glory by keeping His covenant of love.

Let us not stumble in the darkness when there is Light attainable. The rainbow is the hinging together of all colors. Let our many races be brought together to reflect the love of God.

Today: I don't worry much about what makes the rainbow. Some days my biggest problem is to believe that there are rainbows. Just as it takes both rain and the sun to make a rainbow, so it takes both ups and downs to make a good day. What's important is how I respond to my ups and downs. The world will be influenced by how I live my life. That's a staggering thought—and I'm going to make myself believe it. This old world is better or worse because of how I live this day. Wow!!

Melting

They really scared me as they stood way up on the snow piled high by the plow. Each was throwing snowballs at the passing cars. I was positive either one would lose his footing and fall in front of an automobile.

One missile hit my windshield as I parked the car. Roman collar and all I scrambled after the fleeing culprits. They knew the area well. Over a yard fence, through a garage, through a gate, across an alley they led me.

In the side door of another garage and they were trapped. They were guilty urchins when the chase had begun but now that they were cornered their guilt had grown immensely. My shoes were full of melting, cold snow. My trousers had been torn going over the fence. A low limb had nearly taken off my head.

"What is your name?" No answer. "Don't you know you could get hurt or hurt someone else throwing snowballs?" No answer, no nods—nothing.

"O.K. If I have to go through this whole neighborhood, I'm going to find your mothers and talk with them."

"Please," said the older child, who looked about seven or eight. "My name is Timmy. I live over there. But please don't take Bill to his mother. She is really mean to him and it was all my fault."

My wet feet, torn trousers and bruised head suddenly were insignificant compared to the lump in my throat. "Tell you what. You promise not to throw anymore snowballs and I'll forget the whole thing. O.K.?" "Gosh yes. Anything to save Bill. He's my friend."

Today: Talk about peace movements! The snowball episode ended in what one could call a peace movement. Does one need to encounter a mean person before one agrees to PEACE? There's a song that begins with: "Let there be peace on earth, and let it begin with me."

If oursiders look "in" on me, do they recognize me as a peace lover? as a peace maker?

Today I'll study the peace in my own heart. If there's going to be peace in this world, it's got to start with me.

Before the Ancients

The teacher in the C.C.D. class had discussed the notion of God. He is eternal, everywhere, all powerful. Each attribute was carefully outlined for the little children.

Each had something to say about his own concept of God. Each sat in awe of the other's words of wisdom. All was accepted with childlike faith.

It was thrilling just to think God could be everywhere—inside and outside of everyone. He was where no one else has ever yet been and where people could never go.

And He had always been everywhere. Always. Always is a long time. God was older than anyone's grandparents. No one was older than God.

As each student took paper and crayon to draw pictures and print words, it was obvious that one child was concerned. He knew how some people get when they age. They become confused and feeble. They don't always understand and appreciate little people. And these people were young compared to God.

Suddenly, the child began to print—large and deliberate letters. His jaw was set. He was determined in God's favor. The teacher collected the words and pasted them on the wall.

A smile crossed her face as she read the words the child had traced: "God may be old, but He can still lick Satan!"

Isn't it strange how man thinks God is old because He is eternal? God is not eternally old, He is eternally young.

Today: God!! What does that word really mean? Thinking about that one word will keep one busy all day—every day.

Moses worked on behalf of God and His people. I just wonder if Moses knew God better than I do? How does one come to know God? How did Moses get to know God? Oh, yes, he went to the mountaintop, he went to the desert.

Today I will go in search of God—to the mountain— through the desert.

A Pleasure

Living for the moment is sometimes quite difficult living. "The evil of the day is sufficient," especially when one is unprepared for the evil.

The preparation for a day of fun, fun, fun is never adequate. Man just isn't designed for fun, fun, fun.

If the high schooler loves and lives basketball he still eventually finds out from his blisters that he better sit down and quit the game, at least temporarily.

The food an adult cannot stomach is often the same food in which he, at some time in life, overindulged.

It isn't unusual that persons who plan "the greatest party ever" can very likely fade out with, "This is the last time I ever want to have this much fun!"

Too much fun isn't fun at all. Too much fun is extremely painful. Moderation and temperance are still and always will be important ingredients in happy living. Unfortunately, temperance demands experience as both parents. Eventually experience begets moderation even for the slowest learners.

Playwright George Bernard Shaw says it well: "Isn't it too bad that youth is wasted on the young?" Youth could be used so much better by the experienced old man with not money but—temperance. The second time around I think youth would last much longer—and be more fun.

Today: Human beings, including me, are really puzzling beings. Today with its pleasure—its joy, love and happiness—is barely over and I wonder what tomorrow will bring. Each yesterday is so quickly forgotten and it seems that I'm always on the move.

Between each yesterday and tomorrow is *today*—a real today. Thanks, Lord, for today. I love it—every minute of it and when today becomes a yesterday, I'll still love it because it came from you, sweet Lord.

I'm determined—I mean it—I'll never live for tomorrow again—I'll always live just for today. I'll be glad that there is a today.

Unimportant Problems—Unimportant Person

One of the greatest problems in life can be a lack of problems. A man with no problems is hardly a person. Every decision, every relationship, every venture poses a problem.

This may seem pessimistic but it isn't at all. A man who decides to marry should be aware of at least some difficulties involved in his new role as husband and father. Unless he has enough love to accept both the good and the bad possible in marriage, he should continue accepting the present problems of the single life.

Faith, hope and love are essentials in life. If I lack confidence in self and others, then my problems are too much to handle. If I have no hope in the future for happier times, then I have the real problem of despair. If there is nothing worth loving in life, then we are blind to reality. The fact is, we cannot imagine living without some faith, some hope and some love.

If I have the worry of giving a good sermon, I also have the joy of knowing people will be present. If no one ever came to Mass, I surely wouldn't be concerned about preaching—at least not in church.

If I worry about getting money to the bank, I also have the pleasure of knowing I have money. If I am concerned about feeding a family, I know I'm of extreme importance to everyone under the roof called home.

Our best friendships are often formed when we are down and out. Misery loves company—especially when company removes misery. Problem-solving is a rewarding thing. If I'm really living, God knows what problems I may face tomorrow—and how well.

Today: I never gave it much thought before—but company really does remove misery. Others can lead us out of darkness when we can't find our way. The company of others, too, can take away our fears and even help make pain seem like pleasure.

Today I'm going to do some more thinking about the joy of being in the company of others. Every human encounter can help open the door to the Divine

Presence. I won't forget either that some days I'm good company for myself, too. Some days my vision is clear—my perception is sharp and it's good to be with myself. Thanks, Lord, for making me "not so bad" after all.

The Prodigal

We so often hear the parable of the prodigal son that we have come to think the word "prodigal" means to return. The word actually means spendthrift or waster.

What is particularly interesting in the parable is the fact that the real spender is first and last the father—not the son. It is the father who foolishly gives the son his share of the inheritance long before he is prepared to know how to handle it.

On his return, the son is greeted by the father and given a more than splendid banquet. So splendid in fact that the elder son is outraged.

The fact is, the parable is consistent with life. God, our father, is very much a prodigal. He gives all of us so many talents and abilities which we neither develop nor use. Or if we do use them, we so often use them foolishly, in such a way that they serve not the purpose of God or man.

It is almost as though God continues spoiling us in spite of Himself. We have too much. If we had only our sight, how well we would use our eyes. If we had only our hearing, with what caution we would protect our ears. How careful is the unsighted deaf person even with his sense of touch.

We are allowed to go through life wasting our wealth and riches in selfish ways. Yet, our Father is ever watchful for our return to reality and His table.

What He gives us in this life is as nothing compared to His final prodigality—eternal love and joy with the Eternal Spendthrift—who spent even His own Son for our eventual return.

Today: It seems that the real problem for most of us is the same as it was for the prodigal son. How does one preserve integrity and freedom at the same time? We are all prodigal in one way or another. So let's stop talking about THE prodigal son and take a good look at ourselves. At least, that's what I'm going to do today—try to figure out how to keep myself from being so prodigal! Maybe it's beyond the realm of possibility for the likes of me, but then there is such a thing as the return of the prodigal so there's hope for me! And you!

More Prodigal

When the elder son protested to the father that there should be no banquet for his prodigal brother, the father responded in magnificent fashion: "We had to celebrate the return of your brother. He was lost and has been found."

Life is full of necessities. Much fuller than we generally realize or appreciate. We limit the necessities to eating, drinking and sleeping. Things that seem most essential to survival.

To survive as humans and not mere animals there is the beautiful necessity of celebration. The prodigal son had lived like an animal. He had sunk so low he was not allowed to eat with the swine.

His restoration demanded celebration. Human life demands celebration. So often our daily existence has become so routine that we forget this fact. So often we act and react like Pavlov's dog that we fail to celebrate because no one else pushes the buttons in life which say: rejoice, be glad, celebrate!

Thank God that for most of us there are moments when all the right ingredients are brought together and in spite of ourselves we must dance, we must sing, we must laugh.

One must wonder how often all the ingredients are present, yet we react like the elder brother who refuses to dance, sing and laugh. The younger son's return cost the elder nothing. He had more reason to rejoice than the father. The difference was found in one circumstance—attitude.

How often are we in situations wherein we "have to celebrate" and refuse to do the human thing. Let us constantly rise above mere animal nature and celebrate with the Father of the human race.

Today: Basically healthy people have the capacity to celebrate life. It is the unhealthy who become rigid and institutionalized. The less rigid one is, the greater is his/her capacity to celebrate—even to celebrate the return of the prodigals.

A great mark of holiness is to be able to rejoice with those who rejoice—or with those who return to their Father. Someday, that return will be a real return for each one of us. Today I'm actually going to celebrate my death day—I might not be able to when it really happens so I'm going to do it now—today. Someday I'm going back to my Father!

Enough Love?

It is difficult to find any pleasure in anything that is spoiled—especially when the spoiled is a human being. To keep anything from spoilage there is demanded a just-rightness.

If fruit becomes too heated or too cold it spoils quickly. If a child—or adult—receives too much or too little attention it also can easily spoil.

There cannot be too much love, but there can be too much of what may be mistaken for love. If love is infinite, as John tells us it is, then its increase is always desirable. Any substitute for love is truly unfortunate.

If a spouse is jealous, it is a difficult situation that can easily reach tragic proportions. A "jealous lover" "loves" only himself and he is a spoiled person who can easily destroy any possibility of real love.

A child who is given "everything" generally is given everything but love. Love may be at first sight but it requires a lifetime of development. Love is full time or it is not at all.

Love takes many forms and is sometimes hard to diagnose. It can come with kisses or spankings. It can sweep you off your feet or go unnoticed. Love is strange because in spite of its greatness, and sometimes because of it, it demands no recognition or reward.

Love is never blind nor will it close its eyes to the faults of the loved. Love demands perfection and does not rest until it is reached. It always strives for greatness—love's eyes are always open for opportunities.

Greatness is fostered by love. If being spoiled is the result of a lack of greatness, it is thereby the result of love not given or received. A spoiled generation cries out for love—a healthy generation is living it.

Today: Being spoiled is a sort of sickness—there's some kind of unfulfilled psychological need in the spoiled person—God forbid that it ever be so with religious men and women. Such spoiled persons cannot respond wholeheartedly to the Spirit. Let's pray for priests and sisters so their own needs never master them. This is a plea for religious men and women to refrain from becoming spoiled—but to remain unentangled with self and to continue to see others instead.

From spoiled priests and sisters, deliver us, O Lord!

Slavery, Self Imposed

Since the Church has allowed so much freedom it is easily seen that many were not ready for it. Freedom demands a great deal more intelligence and diligence than slavery.

In the past, when so much morality was legislated, it was easy to merely follow directions and be saved. Now, when one must decide for himself, within the realm of his own conscience, it is easy to become confused.

To throw off shackles does not constitute freedom. To quit eating meat on Friday was a good regulation. One was reminded every day of Christ because he had to ask, "Is today Friday?"

This regulation was discarded with the hope that each Catholic could decide for himself what he might do to discover some more meaningful way to express his relationship with Christ.

Unfortunately for some they have done nothing to maintain, much less develop, meaningful ways for such relationships. They have thrown off Christ-centeredness with the "shackles."

Each of us has the intelligence to find better means of closeness to our Savior. Our consciences easily guide us in this matter. Our background insists on such formation.

The real problem is that of diligence. We take not the time nor the the energy to even consider the various methods attainable to encourage spirituality. Our diligence is so lacking that even the word spirituality leaves us cold.

Our intelligence can easily become stagnant due to lack of diligence and we can become slaves unto ourselves instead of the Church—and our last state is much worse than the first.

Today: Progress must not be such a great thing if "to make progress" means to throw off shackles and demand one's freedom. I just can't figure out what is so great about that kind of freedom. Since we are all headed for the "resurrection of the body" the day is coming when we'll all be free. Then it won't make much difference which way the altar in the church was facing or whether the music during the Communion was an organ or a guitar solo. Renewal must be a reality, but I'm beginning to wonder what it all means. Why do so many people who write and talk about renewal sound as if we've all been slaves and that renewal is an escape from slavery. It seems to me that faith makes me free . . . at least my kind of faith does. How about yours?

Live and Let Live

There is either a growing number of people who think "mercy killing" is good and necessary or the number has become much more vocal.

So there is no danger of being murderers by intent, a general admonition is added to their conversations. "Only in extreme cases. When it is for their own good. Only when it is for the good of society. In case they are mentally-deranged"—and so on.

Sometimes, of course, there is the final washing of hands with the understanding that a panel of experts or the government would be the judges.

It is amazing that the pushers for mercy killing are generally against capital punishment. They would rather kill the innocent than the guilty.

History has allowed "mercy killing" for almost every human situation. If one were to sit and write five things which describe himself he might be amazed to find that some time in the past, or in the present, man has killed man for being one or all the five things.

Jews and gentiles have killed one another. Blacks, whites, reds and yellows have taken turns at murder. The Crusades pitted Christian against Moslem. Communists have killed capitalists and vice versa. Spanish Conquistadors killed Indians for being pagans. Some cultures allow fathers to put to death any daughter merely on whim.

One could go on, but the list is long enough. In no case are we talking about sin or human failure in the above list. They are situations generally beyond the individual's control. And in each case the governing body sponsored the legislation rather than merely allowing it.

To live is a basic human tendency. Let us at least keep the basics in civilization or we won't have a civilization.

Today: God's work in this world depends upon me—it depends upon you and upon every man, woman and child in this world. It is not enough for us to live and let live but while we are doing that, love must be the vital sign. Only love shows that we are about God's work in this world.

The quality of our love determines the quality of our life. What a thought! Today I won't just live and let live but I'll test the quality of my love. I won't stop until I've reached my greatest potential to love. Love gives life—real life!

Yes, Yes, Lukewarm a No-No

"Mom, I could just die, I want to go so much. Please let me go to the movies." Such pleading is not an unusual thing. The request may be legitimate. The decision is mother's.

"Look dear, if 'no' kills you, then don't ask. It's like suicide. You know how I feel about movies on a school night."

Sometimes, the offspring can take another approach: "If you don't want to hear 'no'—don't ask." That can be a dangerous approach.

Whether parents are lenient or strict seems to be of less importance than their being consistent. When the same question gets a pleasant "yes" on Tuesday and a gruff "no" on Friday, the youngster has to be confused.

Permission shouldn't be granted or refused on the basis of the tide or how the cookie crumbles unless you live on the beach or own stocks in the bakery.

Not too long ago I heard a college student, who had been raised by a very authoritarian father, say, "I always know where I stand with dad. In fact when I was younger he was often the reason why I would stand. As I grow older he stands higher in my mind. No matter how strict he was I knew he was doing things for my good, even though he was sometimes wrong. And when he realized he had been wrong he was always willing to apologize."

If parental love is constant so also is the authority in the home. If one establishes love, authority is present. Authority based on force, fear or error is no authority at all. It is slavery. Let there be a consistent love.

Today: Parents are such models for their children. There is nothing vague and uncertain about it. Mom and dad can help resolve conflicts, whether they are conflicts of growth or change, of development or progress. Every child likes to look at that one man and say, "That's my pop."

An appropriate relationship between parents and children can be a source of grace and a channel of peace.

God grant that all parents learn to say yes, yes and no, no in just the right way at the right time.

I hope parents love their children before it is too late and children love their parents before they see the coffin get closed. Sometimes it is just too late.

When love is present, authority ceases to be the problem.

Acceptability

Christ talks about the Old Law being imperfect as contrasted with the New Law which is perfect. The Old was based on justice—the New on love.

One day, when I was still in high school, I sat on the back porch shining my shoes. My mother came out and we talked about many unimportant things. As I completed my task, she asked me a question: "What is her name?"—and so I told her.

For a long time I wondered how she knew there was someone. Suddenly, the light came through. For years under the old law of obedience I left my shoes quite dirty. Now the law of love demanded a new perfection.

The youngster who has never cleaned anything in his life one day comes home with a date and is suddenly embarrassed: "Gosh, Mom, this house is an awful mess!" The mother has mixed emotions. He has attained many of the attributes she has begged for but she's not too impressed with the girl.

Perhaps the key is acceptability. At home, the child knows his parents love him, clean or dirty. He is about as acceptable as he wants to be and then some. Suddenly his need to impress someone comes sharply into focus. All the heretofore unheeded pleadings of mother and dad become heeded and what seemed to be futile is now realized. The new law of love has taken over.

It would be a tragic existence if one never felt the desire for acceptability, when no one really would care if one proved himself or not. It would be an eternal tragedy if one never knew how much Christ longs for his acceptability. Let us live in the New Law.

Today: What a thought—the law of acceptability! Why does there have to be a law to force us to accept one another?

> One of the greatest cravings of the human heart is to be accepted—yet there is so much rejection in this world. I wonder why people have to have polished shoes in order to be accepted. I guess we place so much emphasis upon the body, clothes and looks. God forbid that my friends feel accepted only because of how they look.

Today I'm going to re-examine the reasons why I love my friends. There must be something more to friendship than looks and clothes.

I'll spend some time today thinking about the beauty of the human person. What makes my friends so lovable— I'm sure it's not polished shoes and hair spray.

Man—Still Human

There seems to be something in man which allows him to spend much more time considering his failures than his successes. I once talked with a fellow who had won over five hundred dollars playing poker. His reaction was normal: "On the biggest pot of the night I lost to a bigger full house. I would have really cleaned up if I'd won that one."

A college football player set a new individual rushing mark in the conference for one game. He summed the day up quite nicely: "On that play where I was stopped on the one foot line I should have scored the winning touchdown." His mind was focused not on all his gains, but his inability to gain one more specific foot.

We all set goals for ourselves which we never attain. The housewife plans to bake bread. All day she works at a myriad of tasks. Her whole time is spent fruitfully. At bedtime she bemoans the fact that the oven's breakdown ruined the bread.

Even when one performs every self-appointed task he can be disappointed because he didn't plan more things when he is obviously so competent. Eventually he will assign performances he cannot attain.

This is not to say he is bound to be a pessimist about life and living. Indeed, he is an optimist. He continues making plans he cannot fulfill. The man who plans nothing and accomplishes the same is the pessimist.

I wonder if our subconscious might be striving for a perfection our conscious is really not expecting. I wonder if imperfect man is not actually always reaching for the perfect—the image in which God created him.

Today: Some of the worst words I hear people say are, "I should have," "I wonder what if" and "why didn't I." It takes a great deal of courage to live life without *ifs* and *buts*. It's often easier to live life in retrospect than to live in the future. It might help if I could actually realize that I am human and consequently there will be mistakes. Who wants to be perfect, anyway?

Believe it or not—today I'm actually going to thank God for my imperfections—after all, I actually do believe I could be worse.

Let Him be God

Prayer is a conversation with God. It is a conversation in which we adore, thank, petition or ask forgiveness. Usually, however, prayer takes the form of a petition.

For many people, it is difficult to adore God because there is the possibility of only one God and most think they are God. The same thing is true of thanksgiving—whatever we have that is good, we credit ourselves.

And insofar as asking forgiveness—here too what need have we when we live in a society where anything goes? Where nothing is sinful?

It seems the only time that we really give God His due is when we are asking for something. There is in the prayer of petition an indication that maybe we aren't God and that He alone can provide what we cannot attain by ourselves. Though even in prayer of petition most of us play God. We talk with Him as though we were ordering a meal in a restaurant—and the customer is always right.

How often though, when the ordered meal arrives, even if it be according to request, do we find ourselves dissatisfied—or do we look with a certain envy at what our neighbor took from the menu?

I find I am seldom disappointed when I ask the chef or the waitress, "What is good today?" They seem pleased I trust their judgment—and seldom do they quip, "Everything is good."

If I find it foolish to trust my own judgment and turn to the chef, I wonder if I'm not even more foolish in always telling God what is best for me.

So often in prayer I ask for so little, whereas if I were to tell Him to give me what is best for Him and me, I would discover a more generous God than I could have anticipated. If I don't limit God He can be more easily limitless with me.

Today: I'm going to convince myself that I am not God—that I *never was* God and I *never will be* God.

> I'll let God be God and I'll be me—today. It might even be a relief.

Obedience

It is interesting that Christ, at the age of twelve, was so anxious to begin the work of His Father. He even seemed surprised that Mary did not understand what He meant when He asked, "Did you not know I must be in my Father's house?"

In today's Gospel, when Christ is presumed to be about thirty years of age, His tone has changed. At twelve He was ready to change the world—at thirty He claims "My hour has not yet come."

We can shrug our shoulders and say, "That's life." Young people are always trying to turn the world upside down, but when they mature they become more responsible and cautious. With this presumption we can conclude that Christ fits the pattern.

However, there is a much more important element to be seen on these two occasions and that is the element of obedience. In each instance Christ knows what He wants—and in each instance He does that which His mother requests.

The "Woman wrapped in silence" utters her last recorded words in today's Scripture: "Whatever He asks you to do, do it." She presumes His obedience, but even while presuming it she gives Him total freedom and tells the world to be obedient to Him. If one could follow the advice of her last utterance, he would be perfect.

The Gospel of today's liturgy relates the only miracle worked by Christ that can be considered a luxury miracle. In every other miracle He is working only with essentials. The single luxury miracle recorded is out of obedience to His mother.

Obedience is a key to His entire life. Just as it was by disobedience that man needs a Redeemer—so by obedience are we redeemed. His public life begins as an act of obedience to His mother—it ends in an act of obedience to His Father. In His words, "Not my will, but thy will be done," He is being obedient unto His very death.

Today: I'll stop my rushing around today and think about what it means to say "Not my will, but thy will be done."

If I think about it for awhile I may even conclude that the *Lord's will* is better than *mine*.

The Good Seed

In today's Gospel, Christ indicates that enemies are in existence who will stop at nothing to destroy the effects of good works. It is interesting that the servants of the master and the enemy of the master perform exactly the same task—each sows seed in exactly the same field within hours of one another.

There is a message here which we can easily miss. No matter what kind of life we live—no matter what we do—we are all teachers. There is always someone ready to learn from us whether we do good or evil.

Or perhaps we can take a different perspective altogether—that anytime we are living a life of awareness we have the opportunity of accepting the good seed, the news of salvation. Or we can accept the weed seed, which is for our eternal loss.

The fact remains, in this parable, that the world will always have the good and the bad, side by side. It is impossible to be in the world and not be aware of good and evil about us.

Many of us have been taught to flee evil, but this would be to leave the world completely. In modern society, science would take the bad seed, test it, and determine every good quality it possessed. Then science would try to develop the good qualities to the exclusion of the bad.

In social living the same should hold true. No matter how evil a person may seem, he has good qualities, given by God, which can be developed. As Christians, we can no longer shun those who energetically plant the bad seed, but direct their faculties toward the good of which they are capable.

Parents can no longer say, "Don't play with that child. His mother and father are not socially acceptable." Today, the word must be—"Bring him home with you. Invite him for a meal. Let us share what we have."

Christians must live lives of such happiness and joy that those who sow only the bad seed will be totally ineffective—for the most important thing we have is Christian love.

Today: I will sow my own seed—I will "do my thing" with LOVE.

Maybe I can LOVE so much with my good seed, that I will smother the other seed—the bad seed. Two seeds can't grow in the same place at the same time—may the best seed win!

All I Want for Christmas

At this time of the year we find ourselves wishing one another a very "Merry Christmas." It is good to be able to wish someone anything that is beneficial.

If we are honest we would admit there are certain things we want for Christmas from parents, spouse, children, relatives or friends. We all become somewhat children and wonder if what is under the tree and our title is really what we hope it is.

Suppose now that it is not something a friend or relative can give. Suppose that God the Father were to ask: "What do you want for Christmas?"

I think one would say, "Give me a world full of song, not the singing of angels but of men. Give me a world filled with joy and peace. Give me the things Christ came into the world to bring."

The worry I find when I open a Christmas card and suddenly realize it is from a person I've forgotten sends me scurrying to the post office with a hope of reconciliation—and, whom else have I forgotten?

Christmas is a time to sing. Christmas is a time when armies have a momentary cease fire for a temporary peace on earth. Christmas is a time for joy. Christmas is a time when all the things God wanted and wants for the world happen—unless man wills it otherwise.

The Hebrew nation awaited a Christ whom they failed to recognize. The same Christ is awaiting recognition today. Is it possible that His birthday can have so little meaning—real meaning—His meaning in our Christmas?

Today: What do I want for Christmas? Each year I get asked that same question and each year I try to please others by making a "want" list. It does make their Christmas shopping easier, they say.

This year I'll be honest and admit that I really don't have any wants of my own. I'll suggest that my friends give to charity instead. I wonder how much money we could collect if all those of us who really don't have any needs, redirected our gifts to the really poor. I'll try and hope that someone plays "follow the leader."

Happy New Day

The New Year's beginning is a creation by the mind of man to celebrate on one day what Christ wants us to celebrate every day. Now we look back to the past twelve months and examine our successes and our failures. We look ahead to determine how we can increase the former and remove the latter.

The Church asks us to do this daily in the Liturgy of the Mass and regularly in the sacrament of reconciliation.

We are asked as Christians to constantly renew the face of the earth. This includes some individual face lifting also.

We prepare to celebrate now an entire year—and some people try to squeeze in a year of celebrating! Christ wants us to celebrate every day in the same spirit of joy that we try to generate during this season.

Let our celebration not be one designed to forget the past. Let it be one designed to enrich the future.

Today: I just got an idea. Every morning when I arise during the new year I'm going to look at myself in the mirror and say "Happy New Day." I'm going to mean it, too.

Besides that I'm going to try to get others to do it—to mean it—to try it. Look at yourself tomorrow morning, amid toothpaste and all and say—"Happy New Day."

MEMOS

MEMOS

MEMOS

Father Paul F. Halloran, ordained for the Diocese of Winona in 1953, received his present appointment as pastor of St. Bernard's Church in Stewartville, Minnesota, in 1975. During the intervening years he had served in Winona, Mankato, Good Thunder, and Pipestone. Rural life, related issues and problems are a major concern of Father Halloran, who was named diocesan director of Rural Life in 1973. He has since been elected to a two-year term as president of the diocesan directors of the National Catholic Rural Life Conference.

Father Halloran, a native of Canton, Minnesota, has been an active member of several organizations, including the American Legion which he served as Department of Minnesota chaplain. While chaplain of the St. Thomas More Newman Center at Mankato State University he had the distinction of becoming the first Catholic priest in the nation ever to serve on a YMCA board. Another interest has been the problem of drug abuse, a concern which led to his involvement in rehabilitation work.

Among a number of other appointments, Father Halloran is a member of the newly established diocesan pastoral team. Despite a busy schedule he still finds the time to give retreats and missions— and, of course, to write. This book is the sequel to his first, *A Little Wine*, published in 1974. Both books are collections of articles originally written for weekly church bulletins. His writing also includes "Wagging Tongues," a pamphlet on gossip, and, another reflection of his interest in rural life, "Farm Pen," a column for The Courier, the diocesan newspaper.